D0248857

the known,

the secret,

the forgotten

the known,
the secret,
the forgotten

A MEMOIR

JOAN WHEELIS

W. W. NORTON & COMPANY

Independent Publishers Since 1923

New York | London

From LOOK HOMEWARD, ANGEL by Thomas Wolfe. Copyright © 1929
by Charles Scribner's Sons. Copyright renewed © 1957 by Edward C. Aswell,
Administrator, C.T.A. and/or Fred W. Wolfe. Reprinted with the permission of
Scribner, a division of Simon & Schuster, Inc. All rights reserved.

For information about permission to reproduce selections from this book,
write to Permissions, W. W. Norton & Company, Inc.,
500 Fifth Avenue, New York, NY 10110

For information about special discounts for bulk purchases, please contact
W. W. Norton Special Sales at specialsales@wwnorton.com or 800-233-4830

Manufacturing by Worzalla Publishing Company
Book design by Chris Welch
Production manager: Beth Steidle

Library of Congress Cataloging-in-Publication Data

Names: Wheelis, Joan, author.
Title: The known, the secret, the forgotten : a memoir / Joan Wheelis.
Description: First edition. | New York : W.W. Norton & Company, [2019]
Identifiers: LCCN 2018057904 | ISBN 9781324002581 (hardcover)
Subjects: LCSH: Wheelis, Joan. | Psychoanalysts—United States—
Biography. | Women psychoanalysts—United States—Biography. |
Parent and child—Biography.
Classification: LCC BF109 .W44 2019 | DDC 150.19/5092 [B] —dc23
LC record available at https://lccn.loc.gov/2018057904

W. W. Norton & Company, Inc., 500 Fifth Avenue, New York, N.Y. 10110
www.wwnorton.com

W. W. Norton & Company Ltd., 15 Carlisle Street, London W1D 3BS

1 2 3 4 5 6 7 8 9 0

FOR NWG

Remembering speechlessly we seek the great forgotten language,

the lost lane-end into heaven, a stone, a leaf, an unfound door.

Where? When? O lost, and by the wind grieved,

ghost, come back again.

—THOMAS WOLFE, *Look Homeward, Angel*

CONTENTS

the known,

the secret,

the forgotten

destiny

I WAS THE MUCH-WANTED DAUGHTER OF TWO PHYSICIANS who trained in psychiatry and practiced psychoanalysis. They were as different from one another as they were similar.

My mother grew up in Vienna, Austria, and my father in Marion, Louisiana. They were both born in 1915 and their birthdays were twelve days apart. They liked to muse that their respective fathers had fought against each other in World War I.

My father grew up in poverty, my mother in privilege. They met in Massachusetts in 1951. They were both married at the time and my father had two small children. Their illicit love affair was passionate and tormented. It took a long time for them to find their way to one another. Guilt, uncertainty and sadness gripped the beginning of their marriage. I was told that my birth fundamentally changed that.

My parents are both dead, yet their lives are very much within me. Time and memory rushing in like waves on distant shores. Pulling shells and stones and crabs out to sea and then tossing them back to shore again. Loudly and then softly. Inexorably.

My son likes to remind me that he and I are all that is left of my parents. The threads of connection, heritage, legacy. The burdens too. This book is dedicated to him.

daisies won't tell

IN MY HOUSE IN PUGET SOUND IS A LINEN DOILY, WITH A SCAL-loped edge, hand-embroidered flowers, and the words "Daisies Won't Tell." My father's mother, Olive, made it and my father gave it to me. It hangs in the old white house on the wall paneled with Philippine mahogany, once a sea of dark green wallpaper with pink flamingos. The framed doily has not been there long. It moved with me, folded up, from apartment to apartment, and when I had the money, I took it to be properly framed. The framer was unimpressed with the grayed piece of cloth with its irregular shape and slanted hand stitching. He didn't say so, but I could tell by the way he spoke of the expenses involved in framing it, especially the archival glass he thought was a waste of money. I didn't bother to explain to him why it mattered.

In 1908, Anita Owen wrote a song called "Daisies Won't Tell." My grandmother married my grandfather on June 19 of the same year. A love song in the form of a waltz, it became a best seller. Sung by Manuel Romain, it was released as a record in 1910.

> There is a sweet old story you have heard before
> Here among the daisies let me tell it o'er—
> Only say you love me
> For I love you well.
> Answer with a kiss, dear.
> Daisies never tell!
>
> Daisies won't tell, dear.
> Come, kiss me—do!
> Tell me you love me.
> Say you'll be true
> And I will promise always to be tender
> And faithful, sweetheart, to thee!

My father was born October 23, 1915. In 1916 a photograph was taken of him sitting in his father's lap, his older sister, June, sitting on his father's right knee and my grandmother standing behind the three. Behind her is a hearth and, draped over the mantel, the doily with a clock set at ten minutes past eleven.

I can only imagine that my grandparents had heard the love song, maybe even danced to it. It caught the fancy of the young couple, and my grandmother decided to make the doily with its wreath of daisies and the pithy phrase. During the war my grandparents and their two children moved to army camps in Alabama, Mississippi and Tennessee. In 1919 they moved back to Marion, Louisiana. When my grandfather contracted tuberculosis, they moved to San Antonio, Texas, for the drier climate believed to be beneficial for convalescence. My grandfather died in 1925. My father went to college in Austin, ran a theatre in town for a few years and then left Texas to attend the Columbia University College of Physicians and Surgeons in 1936. I do not know when my father took possession of the doily. Perhaps it was after my grandmother died at age one hundred in 1990, a few months after I was married.

Each time I stand in front of the framed doily and look at the century-old photo of my father, I feel a connection to those frozen in time. It is strange and jarring. I feel vitally linked to the past. Time collapses. Fanciful thoughts cross my mind that with the doily, the photo and the right incantation I might step into the past and be with those pictured by the hearth. Or perhaps I could pull them out of the photograph to be with me in the present. Spirits standing with me looking at the doily on the wall.

deer

I HAD A FRIEND FROM THE PACIFIC NORTHWEST WHO TOLD ME
that he felt himself to be a part of the soft, deep paths of
Douglas fir needles, Oregon grape and salal, the frigid waters
of Puget Sound with its seals, seaweed, salmon and jellyfish,
the beach with the sand dollars, herons, ospreys and kingfish-
ers. Once when we went swimming together in the cold, clear
water in the late afternoon sun, he said, "Swimming here I can
feel the spirit of the Sound. We are part of the earth where
time and memory settle." He quoted T. S. Eliot: "We have lingered in the chambers of the sea / By sea-girls wreathed with
seaweed red and brown / Till human voices wake us, and we
drown."

He lived each day as part of the earth he so deeply loved. He died a very old man playing with his grandchildren. We held his memorial service in the woods where the air was moist and rich with the scent of evergreens.

His grandson and I were setting up plastic chairs for the guests when a buck with a huge rack walked by. Slowly, stately, just a few feet away. He seemed to come from nowhere, paused, turned to look at us and then vanished silently into the dense brush as suddenly as he had appeared.

"Do you think that was Grandpa?"

"Yes, I do."

One could hardly say otherwise at a moment like that to a ten-year-old boy, but there was no need to dissemble. We create stories to live by.

time

When winter sags the burdened roof,
When pistol shot is snap of frozen branch,
When, under daggered eaves,
Snow moths gnawing at the darkened pane
Whisper at retreating dreams—

—ALLEN WHEELIS

fire

IT IS DUSK. I'M DRIVING TO OUR HOUSE ON THE ISLAND WHERE
I have spent time all the summers of my life. A beautiful,
special place that holds long, happy memories. The familiar
curves, the rich scent of fern, and moss, cedar and fir; I know
the road so well, its final bend, the mailboxes. I turn down the
driveway.

The gate is locked and I sense that something is wrong.
Terribly wrong. I can't see the white house. I fumble through
the handful of keys to the property to unlock the gate. This is
unnecessary as I can just walk around the fence, but my agitation forces me into ritual.

My God, the house is gone! The ground is black. I get
back in the car and drive down the driveway. The split

towering firs on either side of the house are gone too. My father's study, the barn, the old apple and pear orchard—all gone. Nothing but black earth. I'm sweating and crying. Impulsively I call out, "Mummy?! Daddy?!" frantically realizing that their ashes must be gone too. Their ashes were in the house in two wooden boxes in cobalt blue bags. I am running around looking for something, anything to help me. I feel desperate and my efforts are futile. I run toward the neighboring house. I find that the fire's path has stopped and the woods are again verdant. Suddenly I notice the blue bags on the side of the path. I check. The boxes are still intact with the ashes. I can't believe it. I'm relieved. I haven't lost them.

Night is falling, fast. I feel cold, and my mind is furtively trying to make sense of the devastation and the curious preservation of my parents' ashes. How did this happen? Who took the ashes out of the house? Did the fire start within the old walls or from outside? A careless match on the parched grass? An electrical fire? Did someone start it? Did I?

The dream is repetitive. I wake up with a start each time, disoriented with questions about what matters. I want to dream the sequel but I don't. I want to know what happens next. Do I rebuild the house? The barn and study? Replant the orchard? Do I take the blue bags of ashes with me or toss them into the evening breeze to drift over that charred earth? Do I walk away and start over? Am I trying to reckon with the gift of having and the tragedy of loss or the curse of having and the relief of loss? Is it a sign that what matters will always stay intact but I must brace myself for adversity, sadness, uncertainty and doubt before I can secure it?

The feeling is urgent and pressing.

car games

EACH SUMMER MY FAMILY DROVE FROM SAN FRANCISCO TO
Puget Sound to vacation for the month of August. When school
let out in June, I made a wall calendar of the days until August,
crossing them off with a thick black marker. I used to hang the
makeshift calendar in a prominent position in my room, hoping that its visibility with the sinister black X's might change
my parents' mind as to when we would leave. It never worked.

A week before departing we began preparations. Special
foods and wine were packed, along with clothes, books, puz-
zles and the occasional bowl or cooking pot from the basement. The day before, my mother prepared sandwiches, boiled
eggs, washed grapes, froze freezer packs, and made a thermos
of coffee to be ready early the next morning.

These preparations seemed endless and increased the sense of an epic journey about to begin. The night before we left, all the suitcases, boxes and bags were brought down to the garage. My father considered the space of the trunk and then like a chess player strategically planned his moves. A small suitcase with the necessary items for the first night in a motel was made easily accessible. As well as his black leather briefcase containing a clipboard with a dozen or more pages of Crane's Distaff Linen bond stationery, his fountain pen and a bottle of blue-black ink. Just in case he might be inspired in the motel to capture his musings for his next novel. The AAA maps and travel books, newly ordered each year, were put in the glove compartment.

My first memories of this trip were in a blue Buick Skylark. It took twenty-one hours to drive before Interstate 5 was completed; the journey to our summer home spanned two days and one night in Grants Pass, Oregon.

We left San Francisco early in the morning when it was still dark and cold, but by ten the sun was already high in Northern California and the highway shimmered from the heat rising off the asphalt. The Buick was without air-conditioning. At times we were at a complete standstill. The windows were rolled down, letting in the swirling dust and sultry hot air as backhoes and tractors crisscrossed the road before us. The smell of tar was smoky and sweet. My father drove the entire eight hundred miles himself while my mother sat at his side, feeding him cucumber and ham sandwiches, almonds, cookies, fruit and coffee, entertaining him with conversation to keep him mentally occupied and alert. I sat with my dog, Monty, in the back seat. I couldn't read because I became carsick looking down at a book, and I couldn't talk with my parents because they seemed too far away and it was too noisy from the wind and road construction. I couldn't sleep after the sun reached its zenith because it was too sunny and hot to get comfortable. And while I looked forward all year to this pilgrimage north, it was an agonizingly uncomfortable journey. I never complained openly. For a while I would ask how much farther we had to go, but my father had little tolerance for these questions. After I asked a few times, he stopped answering and suggested that I could study the map if I wanted further information as to our progress. Even with the company of my beloved dog, and a myriad of games counting blue cars, red trucks, black cows or "For Sale" signs, which helped ease the tedium, there was little sustained solace.

My father was unsympathetic to my discomfort. His message was that all good things in life require sacrifice. Anything short of stoic tolerance was regarded as weakness of character and failure of will. So I talked to myself and daydreamed about the magical island in Puget Sound to which we were heading.

The summer of my twelfth birthday was a particularly trying one. Adolescent longings for independence and romantic connection were stirring like water about to boil. Patience was low and emotional lability on the rise. I felt like a trapped wild animal in the back seat with too little room even to pace.

I didn't want to eat, sleep or play with my dog. I was too old for my counting games and I had no desire to talk with my parents. Defiantly I turned my back on them and stared out the back window. We were in Northern California. It was midafternoon and the temperature was over 100 degrees. The road construction was winding down and the highway speed was picking up. I stared into each car we passed, searching for distraction. A Volvo with two kayaks on a rack and a couple engaged in lively conversation, a red Mustang convertible towing a boat with a gray-haired man in a seersucker suit. Having become fascinated with *Harriet the Spy* and the art of investigation, I tried to imagine who these people were and what their lives were like. I was relieved for the new mental stimulation. Then we passed an 18-wheeler. The driver had an easy view into the back window of our Buick. I heard a horn and instinctually turned my gaze up into the cab. A handsome man with a broad smile pulled his horn again and turned on his running lights. He waved and I waved back. And I caught his eye; it was all I needed to send me off into a stirring romantic fantasy. I was excited and felt a foreign and intoxicating sense of power. Had I charmed him to show off? Emboldened by this experience, I now waved and smiled promiscuously. Finally, I had found a solution for my restless boredom.

No sooner had the realization and discovery taken hold, however, than I felt my father's large hand on my back. His gentle but authoritative voice called me, "Joan! Joan!"

"What?"

"Please turn around and face forward so I can talk to you."
I didn't want to but his commanding voice subdued my rebellious ardor. I turned around. My father began speaking. "I noticed you were waving out the back window. It looks like it is fun for you."

Expecting criticism, I felt surprise and pleasure by his comment. "Yes, Daddy. The truck driver pulled his horn and turned on his lights and waved at me!"

"I don't want you to do that anymore."

"Why not?" I was miffed.

"Because you are acting falsely."

What was he talking about? "*No*, I'm not!"

He ignored my outburst and went on. "You are ignoring the context of your behavior. You are in a car and protected by glass and your parents from a real engagement. It creates an illusion of power and intimacy. You are acting in an overly familiar way with a stranger. You would not do that if you were on the street walking and he appeared. There, you would be diffident and circumspect because there are consequences of behavior that would be on your mind. He might misread your intentions. And you must always be accountable for your behavior and not pretend to be something you are not. Otherwise it is self-deception."

I had only the vaguest idea of what he was talking about, but I knew for sure that the pleasure I felt but a few minutes before was gone. It was gone like air out of a popped balloon and I would no longer be waving out the back window.

A year before my father died, he published his last book, *The Way We Are*, dedicating it to me. He wrote in the introduction, "[I]n the evolution from animal life to human life, along with the gain in knowledge and awareness, we have gained also the ability to deceive ourselves. We arrange *not to know* our nature *not to see* what we are up to. Our self-deceptions are so dense, piled on so thick, like layers of paint on a canvas already painted, layer after layer, laid on from school and pulpit and lectern and TV and Internet, that it is all but impossible to break through, to get a clear view of what we really are" (p. 16).

When I had finished reading the book, I commented to him, "You've been working on these ideas a long time."

"Well, I suppose I have."

"Forty years! Remember the trucker who honked and waved at me? And how you lectured me about the perils of self-deception?"

"I most certainly do remember."

"I really had no idea what you were talking about then."

"Well, clearly, you do now. And in case you forget, you have an entire book to remind you!"

poppies

I GREW UP IN SAN FRANCISCO. AT POINT REYES IN THE SPRING-time the poppies and lupines bloomed alone the coastline. A brilliance of orange and purple cascading down the hillside to the national seashore. I went there many times with my parents and a blanket, a picnic and the newspaper. We would eat, read, sleep and walk. Sometimes we would hike up from the beach to the headlands. The beauty was spectacular—the flowers, ocean, sky and sun. The vista was so vast that at times I felt I could see the curve of the earth where the ocean met the sky.

As a child, these outings often occasioned questions to my father about existence and belief.

"Daddy, doesn't it seem like this incredible scene just can't be random?"

"It is very beautiful but it's random."

"Why? How do you know?"

"I believe in evolution."

"There's no reason that it should be so beautiful unless it was designed to be that way."

"Well, I think it's possible that it just evolved into this. We are lucky that we are here to enjoy it."

My father's wealth of knowledge was comforting and made me feel safe. These conversations, however, left me uneasy. I liked neither the questions nor the answers. I kept looking for something else.

velvet cap

BY THE TIME WE REACHED THE FERRY LANDING WHERE WE would cross the Sound to the magical island, my excitement was so great I felt short of breath. Monty also knew where we were and started to leap across me from window to window, panting and sniffing the cool sweet air off the Sound. The captain of the eight-car ferry always blew his horn to greet us for our arrival in August. We got out of the car, and I leaned over the side railing, staring into the deep sapphire blue water. After crossing the half mile of Sound, we backed up a steep hill and then set forth on the last leg of our journey across the island. While the pressure in my chest made me long to drive faster, my father drove across the island unusually slowly. One reason was that the two-lane road was narrow and there were hairpin turns, and another was that there were deer.

"Daddy, can't we go a little faster?"

"No."

There was something poignant in the way he said "no" that made it clear there was more to it than the deer and the narrow road. I came to understand that he wanted to savor the end of our pilgrimage like a small, rare, delicious chocolate truffle. With the inevitable arrival in paradise being imminent, the pleasure was so intense that prolonging the journey only heightened the experience. There were three stop signs in the five miles from the west side of the island to the east. Sometimes the road was straight and flat and sometimes it twisted up and down like a roller coaster. In some places sunlight flooded the road and in others it dappled the leaves in the dense forest. There was Douglas fir, cedar, hemlock, alder and maple and a vast undergrowth of huckleberry and salal. The scent of pitch from the towering Douglas fir and the deep aroma of moss and ferns were intoxicating.

The last turn took us onto a mile of dirt road, dust billowing out behind the car, obscuring any definition of the landscape behind. My father drove this last mile even slower. Monty was ready to jump out the window. Before us the trees were majestic—often five feet wide at the base and towering a hundred feet or more toward the heavens. The last few turns were the tightest and my father crept around them, honking to make sure there was no harm coming our way. And then at last the turn down the driveway opening out on the white house and the Sound beyond.

Finally the car doors opened and Monty raced into the tall grass of the orchard, jumping and rolling in delight. We always walked to the front of the house before unloading the car, taking in the beautiful vista of a still Sound and the peninsula beyond. Herons cruised at the shoreline and seal heads bobbed up and down. It was quiet and magical. Standing by my father, I turned to see his expression of solemn homage. It was here he could write. For me it was an enchanted world where I felt exquisitely and mysteriously connected with the essence of life.

The nights were what brought me closest to spiritual reckoning and wondering about Providence. Far from any city, the night sky looked like a black velvet cap—plush soft nap with twinkling stars like sequins. Shooting stars like thread across the bias. The Big Dipper was over the house, Orion's Belt over the Sound. It was looking up that made me think there might be some majestic something else out there beyond our humble existence.

"How far does the sky go?"

"What do you mean, sweetie?"

"I mean, where does it stop?"

"It doesn't. It's infinite."

I directed my gaze downward and leveled my eyes into my father's. I felt the hair on the back of my neck stand up; I could not understand the concept of an infinite sky.

I was eight years old, sitting on my father's lap in front of the white house, perched above the Sound. The water was still except for the small lapping waves at the shoreline. Other than the occasional squawk of a blue heron, the night was silent. Dark and moonless. My eyes turned upward into the black vaulted space above. "How do you know?"

"That's what the scientists have figured out."

"Daddy, is there a God?"

"Some people think there is and others don't."

"Well is there or isn't there a God?"

"Like I said, sweetie, some people think there is and others don't."

"What do you think, Daddy?"

"I don't think there is a God."

"But how do you know?"

"I don't."

"But if you don't know, why do you think there isn't one?"

My father tenderly put his arm around me. "Well, that is what belief is all about. Some people believe in things even when there is no proof that what they believe in is true, and others believe in things that can be known. I am a doctor and I think about things in terms of science and medicine."

"Daddy, do you believe in heaven?"

"No. I have seen many dead bodies and I think when you are dead that is the end of existence."

"But what if there was a spirit of a person that left the body when it died?"

"Well, I don't believe in that."

"But you don't know that it isn't true!"

"No, I don't."

"When I look into the sky, it looks like the inside of a velvet cap and there must be another side to it. I think the scientists should figure out how to get there."

"Sweetie, it's getting cold and I think it's time to go inside and go to bed."

We walked around to the back of the house so my father could take stock of the "velvet cap" in the open area by the orchard away from the towering firs. Staring up, we walked through the dry grass, looking north along the island's perimeter toward the Olympic Mountains. Shooting stars crisscrossed the inky sky.

"Look, Daddy, there is the Big Dipper!"

"Yes, and the north star. In 1958 your mother and I saw *Sputnik* from this very spot. *Sputnik* was a satellite launched into orbit around the Earth by the Soviet Union."

I was more preoccupied with the thought that I was standing so close to my father and could feel his warmth and hear his breath. I felt both flushed and chilly. It seemed so intimate. As my father was teaching me about *Sputnik*, a cool, dry breeze swept up off the slough near the beach, passing over us like a wave. There was something distinct in the air and my father stopped speaking. Above the slough, yellow and green light started to move and take shape like a giant wall of slow, undulating curtains. I stopped breathing and felt again flushed and chilly. I had never seen anything like it. It was fantastic and I blinked my eyes several times to make sure it really was there.

"Look at that! Isn't that marvelous! That's the northern lights, or aurora borealis. It's where the solar wind plays with the Earth's electromagnetic field. It is rare to see it."

"Daddy, doesn't *this* make you think there is a God?"

"No."

I wished I hadn't asked.

"But I do think I see what you mean that the sky looks like a wonderful velvet cap. But I am very cold now and I think we have had enough discussion for tonight."

The shimmering veil of light had vanished into the night sky. I have never seen it again.

blue door

GRASPING WHAT MY PARENTS DID FOR A LIVING WAS A CHAL-lenge for a long time. My parents, both psychiatrists and psychoanalysts, had their offices in our home. There were five floors from the street level of the garage and wine cellar and sixty-three steps to climb to reach the locked wrought-iron gate and the main entrance. Like a castle. Patients climbed the first seventeen steps to the first turn, where there was a blue door. My parents buzzed in their patients through this entry. The waiting room was immediately to the left of another flight of internal stairs. If they were going to see my father, he would walk out of his office and stand at the top of the stairs, the noise of double doors opening alerting the patient in the waiting room that he was ready. My mother would buzz again for her patients, who would climb the same steps to my father's office and then at the landing open the orange door of a two-person elevator. From there the patient traveled past the fourth floor of our house where the living room, kitchen and dining room were and finally to the top floor where my mother's office and our bedrooms were. Separating the house from her office was a three-inch-thick solid oak door.

My parents' bedroom was directly above the dining room. Both rooms were rounded and together projected out from the main structure like a turret. From one of the casement windows in the bedroom, one could see the San Francisco Bay in the distance as well as across an outdoor courtyard into the window of my mother's office and to the chair in which she sat. A window shade was pulled up from the bottom just high enough to cover her head. Occasionally the shade was not raised high enough and I could see the top of her head as she sat with her patients.

My father's office was more hidden. Originally his office had been two smaller servants' quarters and as such was more removed from the main living area of the house. Walking past the blue door and up another flight of external stairs one could see the large curtained windows of his office, but they were set back beyond bush and tree plantings. My father's office had one other window that looked directly out on the final run of stairs to the gate and front door of our house. My father sat in a chair that was directly across from that little window, which had a curtain transparent enough to allow him to make out shape and movement on the steps yet appeared opaque from the outside. There was one other important place in our castle for viewing my father's office. Just past the elevator landing by my father's office, one could pass through a door into the basement of the main house. Elevated above the floor of the basement was a three-foot-high storage area. At one end of the space was a small opening with wood lattice across it, which looked directly out at the door to my father's office. But I did not have all this information for a long time.

This architectural maze made the experience of my parents' livelihood into a profoundly intriguing mystery of endless interest to me. As a little girl, I heard the sounds of the excursions in the elevator and the opening and closing of doors every fifty minutes. But I never saw anyone nor did I hear any voice. Once at the dinner table I asked what a patient was and my mother responded that patients were people who had problems and came to see my parents to help them solve their problems. Not long after, I was returning from the market with my mother and I saw a woman coming out of the blue door. When I inquired, my mother told me that this was one of my father's patients. And then in my six-year-old mind it became clear what was going on: patients were invisible. They came to their appointments in some form like a ghost and my parents made them visible. That explained the silence as the invisible patients made their excursions in the elevator and then *seeing* the person walking down the steps from the blue door.

Several years later while rummaging around in the basement, I heard the sound of doors opening. I rushed over to the small, latticed sash that offered a view of my father's office door. Indeed, the double doors of my father's office were both ajar. My heart was pounding. I felt I had discovered an illicit treasure. By then I had realized that patients were visible both coming and going. Perhaps because I felt guilty about my spying, I was often mixed up as to the times that my parents' patients came and went and so missed sighting them. I had fantasies of a patient seeing me and reporting me to my parents. I imagined my mother's indignation and my father's disappointment that I could be so morally bankrupt.

My father wrote in the morning and then saw five patients after lunch, from 1:30 to 6:20, with ten-minute breaks between them. My mother saw patients all day starting at 8:10 (9:00, 9:50, 10:40, 11:30). Her breaks were the couple of minutes it took for one patient to leave by the elevator and the next to take the elevator up. At 12:20 she joined my father for lunch and then went back at 1:20, ending her day at 6:20.

A devotee of the book *Harriet the Spy*, I carried around a notebook and pencil to document my discoveries. For a long time my experience as a spy primarily consisted of lying under my parents' bed waiting for a glimpse of my mother's Ferragamo shoes or the housekeeper's sandals. Now as a thirteen-year-old sitting in the darkened area of the basement by the latticed opening, I waited to see patients. It was thrilling and made me feel short of breath. I took notes on attire, guessing at age and profession. My mother's patients were often older men with corduroy jackets. My father often saw young attractive women who wore perfume. I kept notes of the days and times they came, noticing that sometimes they came more than once a week. It often felt furtive. I needed to be out of the basement and back up in my room before my mother's break, as she would invariably check in on me in the minute or so she had free. And before my father's break, when he passed through the door by the elevator, along the basement hallway and then up a flight of stairs to the kitchen. He might notice the door slightly open and discover me.

I wondered about the patients' lives, imagined what their problems might be. One of my journal entries read:

> *4:40. Patient to see my mother. Male. Maybe 40–50. Wearing a wedding ring. Hair black, messy, gray short beard. Brown sweater, no jacket, brown corduroy pants and laced tan leather shoes. Impression: Looks sad. Maybe a professor or an architect. His wife works, and does not want children. This makes him sad. He loves her but really wants children. He's an only child.*

My parents never discovered my spying. But shortly before I stopped my undercover reconnaissance, I was startled to recognize a famous pop singer coming up the stairs with her guitar to see my father. She had been an idol of mine and I could hardly believe that I had seen her from just a few feet away, let alone then listened to her sing and play guitar from within my father's office. The exquisite pleasure of the discovery was intoxicating. The subsequent guilt, however, was even more overwhelming and I forever abandoned my post at the latticed sash.

wine

JUST AS WITH CHESS, TENNIS AND ORIENTAL RUGS, MY FATHER became fascinated by and passionate about wine in the late 1950s. He bought books such as *The Noble Grapes and the Great Wines of France* and signed up for the local wine shop's newsletters. Very pleased by the fact that the cool air in the small, high-ceilinged storeroom off our one-car garage was the perfect temperature for storing wine, he had a wine cellar built. Mr. Gudmanson, who did all the fine cabinetry work in our house, fashioned beautiful slatted redwood wine boxes. Enough to hold twenty-five cases of wine, most of which my father bought from two California wine importers: Connoisseur Wine Imports and Kermit Lynch. The door to the wine cellar was kept locked. To camouflage the door and the riches within, my father hung a flattened Beacon Movers garment box on a hook driven into the concrete wall. In the wine cellar, my father kept a hammer and crowbar to open the wooden crates of wine, thermometers, and pens and red tags to label a bottle of each case for easy identification of the wine in their wooden cribs. My father bought most of the wine between 1958 and 1969, and much of it was Bordeaux. The frequency and size of the deliveries began to make my mother fret that he was spending too much money on wine and that they could not possibly consume so much in their lifetime. My father responded to her concerns by scheduling the deliveries to arrive while my mother was seeing patients, and no one went in that room without my father.

When my father died, there were twenty or so bottles, and when my mother died five years later, there were but a few of those left, which were drunk in the last few days before my parents' house on Jackson Street was packed up.

I had been in the wine cellar maybe a handful of times, usually before a big dinner party when I helped my father carry up the bottles that would be served. It was a production to get into the cellar with the cardboard and the locked door. Once inside, the shadowy light of the bare bulb shining through the slatted wood boxes gave the little cool, high-ceilinged room an aura of mysterious secrecy. I often felt that I shouldn't say anything about what I saw in there. After my parents were both dead, the castle was sold. Once the movers drove away with all of my parents' things, I went down to the garage. The cardboard was gone and the door unlocked. I went in; the air felt particularly cold, and my sweater thin. The empty wooden crates made me sad. I don't quite know why I went down, but once there I gathered the tools and the thermometers, and just as I was about to leave, I saw something red out of the corner of my eye. There, tucked off to the side, was a large pile of red tags, each with my father's writing. Forty tags. Among them were the familiar names of the marvelous wines served at my parents' dinner parties:

Pichon-Longueville Lalande '59
Cos D'Estournel '59
Pichon-Longueville Baron '59
Calon-Ségur '61

Many were spectacular wines that we drank in the eighties. The finer they became, the more my mother valued them and wanted to save them. I remember times when my father brought up a bottle of 1961 Château Calon-Ségur, a wine he had bought several cases of on spec in 1959, and my mother would say, "It's too good to drink now." My father, though, for the most part prevailed, claiming that wine, like life, should be lived to its fullest and not be put off for another time. It struck me as an odd reversal of roles, as typically my mother was the more carefree and playful and my father more brooding and inhibited. The last time I drank that wine was in 2004, when my father was eighty-eight. He had recently stopped playing tennis and drank very little wine on account of his irregular heartbeat. I had come home for a visit with my family. He already had the bottle up in the butler's pantry and was starting to open it. "Oh, Daddy," I said. "What a special wine for dinner!"

"It's the last one," he replied. "Over forty years. That's long enough. It may not get any better."

"But it's not even a special occasion," I protested.

"Yes it is. You're here."

the round room

OUR DINING ROOM WAS CIRCULAR. EACH OF THE THREE TALL arched windows parted and opened onto the patio and the gardens beyond of the neighboring mansion, a majestic copy of the Petit Trianon. An arched mirror across from the windows flanked by vases with long branches of quince or willow rendered the impression of yet more gardens on the other side of the room. My father always sat at the head of the table, his back toward a green and white marble fireplace with another arched mirror above the mantel. A simple silver candelabra holding seven candles was at the center of the mantel and a vase of flowers sat off to one side. The room was lit by two ornate wall sconces, each displaying a bouquet of delicate lights under their gilded petals. Japanese, Persian and Italian art hung on the walls between the mirrors. A delicate asparagus fern stood before one of the arched windows. The dark wood parquet floor was adorned by an antique Bokhara rug. There was a Danish sideboard and a small table on wheels and a simple oval teak dining table, which could be expanded to seat twelve. Four burnt orange upholstered chairs, which had belonged to my mother's first husband, flanked the table. It was the epitome of refined yet simple elegance. We ate dinner in that beautiful room each night of the week. I always sat to my father's right facing the mirror, which reflected the gardens behind me, and my parents sat facing one another. My mother, though a marvelous cook, worked full-time and employed a cook to prepare and serve dinner during the week. Veal scaloppini, asparagus, fried eggplant, crêpes Suzette, floating island. And always some wonderful, dark, blood red French wine. While I must have disliked some things served to me, I cannot now recall what those were. My memory in that room was one of endless, undisturbed satisfaction. But those weeknights were nothing compared to the parties my parents held in that room, each of which was an experience of exquisite pleasure for all the senses.

Preparation for a Saturday night party began the weekend before as my mother studied cookbooks to decide on a menu. By Friday night the refrigerator was brimming with things *not* to eat. My parents, like old dance partners, performed their moves with unwavering grace and set about to take care of their respective tasks for the party. My father was in charge of the wine or champagne offered before dinner in the living room and the wine and water served throughout the meal. He also was in charge of writing out the guest names on place cards in the blue-black ink of his Parker fountain pen while my mother decided where everyone would sit. I helped my mother set the table with the starched white Austrian linen, the Riedel crystal, the Valencia plates from Arabia of Finland and the fine Austrian silverware, which had belonged to my Viennese grandmother. The silver chest stood by the front door and was locked with a skeleton key that my mother kept hidden. She was often agitated opening the chest. The silver was indeed valuable and she was afraid of its getting lost or stolen, but her memories were also tied up with the real loss of her parents at the hands of Hitler. She often cried as I helped her set the table. The current of her sorrow flowed through my memories of those occasions and of the exquisitely elegant table with beautiful short stems of fragrant freesia or cedar or jasmine in small glass vases and individual white votive candles in fluted glasses.

When I was invited to join the dinner party, I always sat next to my father. The parties were festive and elegant, and I remember feeling that I was in the midst of the essence of happiness. To sit in the comfortable burnt orange wool-covered chair by my father, gaze upon the flowering branches in the dancing light of candles and eat marvelous things that looked so beautiful and colorful on the dark blue and white plates was magical. My father, infinitely attentive to detail, never let a guest be without water or wine. He never stayed seated and passed the bottle but was up on his feet the moment a last swallow was taken to ensure that his guests felt exquisitely attended to. My mother, always so elegantly dressed and charming, was attentive to the two men at her sides, to the plates of all her guests and to the eyes of my father at the other end of the table. The sound of silverware on china, the movement of water and wine being poured into glasses and the voices of my parents and their guests in that beautiful room settled in my mind like a long night of light snow falling— soft, pleasing drifts of memory accumulating in my mind.

the napoleon

JUST DOWN THE STREET FROM MY DENTIST'S OFFICE AT 1720 Polk was Blum's, a restaurant and confectioner's. And very often following a dental appointment, my father took me there to eat something sweet. It was a naughty and comforting pleasure to eat sugary things after having a cavity filled. We sat at a marble counter with copper edging. All around were the characteristic pink Blum's cans filled with candies like the marvelous almondettes—dark chocolate fudgy chews with a whole roasted almond embedded within. They served coffee and pastries, sandwiches and ice cream. It is difficult to remember exactly what the place looked like, as my senses had already been so overloaded at the dentist's office. What I remember most clearly was what was right in front of me to eat. I loved the burnt almond ice cream and especially loved their napoleons. Also known as mille-feuille, they consisted of six thin layers of crisp puff pastry, each filled with a thick layer of light custard, and the topmost layer had whipped cream under the pastry and a hard, sugary icing with thin lines of symmetrical chocolate swirls on top. The napoleons were served upright on a little paper doily that hugged each side of the pastry. But eating them was a challenge because pressing the fork on the top layer of puff pastry sent custard and whipped cream flying out both sides. The first bite would leave the elegant pastry in shambles.

I can't remember how many napoleons I ate before learning the *right* way to cut one. Probably one or two at most. And after the lesson I never had a messy napoleon on my plate ever again.

I was eight years old. When the waitress brought me the napoleon and a glass of milk, my father said, "Today I am going to show you the proper way to cut a napoleon." He asked the waitress to bring a sharp knife. She was perplexed but obliging. My father's lessons were always memorable because they were delivered as though they had been prepared and rehearsed many times. And probably they had. He thought of every detail, and his arguments were ironclad—at least to me. When the napoleon arrived, he pointed out that the architecture of the pastry was such that trying to cut from the top would put pressure on the layers of custard and whipped cream trapped between the crisp pastry. Turning the napoleon on its side, however, would allow the knife to cut through all six layers of the pastry while minimizing the impact on the custard. He then proceeded to show me. First he laid the pastry on its side, carefully peeling away the half-moon piece of doily. Then he picked up the knife like a scalpel and laid the blade on the napoleon's side, resting against the six layers of puff pastry, whipped cream and icing. He paused to make sure he had my attention and then cut straight down with certain precision. Two equal-size pieces of napoleon lay on their sides, with the layers perfectly preserved. He then instructed me to cut each half as he had done, creating manageable and intact pieces to eat. It took some practice, but after a few cuts I was proficient and my father was satisfied. It seemed of great importance that I had learned this technique. I felt proud to have the knowledge.

When my son was eight, I taught him the technique, noting that he would be the third generation to understand the art of cutting and eating a napoleon. I felt pleased to show him, knowing the expertise would be perpetuated like a master cabinetmaker teaching his apprentice how to make a dovetail joint. When I was done with the explanation and demonstration, he asked, "Why is that better?" I had no good answer.

legacy

WHEN MY FATHER WAS NINE, HIS FATHER WAS DYING OF tuberculosis. My father had received a poor grade at school in conduct, and so his father felt compelled to teach him a final lesson about work and accountability before he died. In the summer of 1924 he asked my father to cut the grass behind their house in San Antonio with a straight-edged razor. It was never entirely clear how large the yard was, but what was clear was that it took my father the entire summer to finish cutting the grass. My grandfather lay in bed with binoculars, watching my father as he worked. He was quick to criticize if he saw any behavior that appeared lazy or careless and would summon my father to his bedside for a lecture. When my father rebelled, my grandfather invoked love as the motivation for his oppressive lesson.

This final punctuation of my father's short relationship with his father was rife with conflict and guilt. By linking love with his brutally harsh expectations, my grandfather left my father longing for approval, and redemption, which he did not receive. My grandfather died shortly after that summer and subsequently my father became serious and disciplined.

He was never really freed of the criticism he internalized, yet my mother, with her proclivity for playfulness and sponta-neity, helped soften the grip.

house in pisa

MY FATHER WAS AN EXACTING MAN—DISCIPLINED, THOR-
ough, orderly—in everything he did. Whenever we traveled
by car to a new place, he studied the map the night before,
determined the best route and memorized it. He wanted no
room for error. The idea of getting lost and pulling over to the
side of the road to take out a map was unpalatable to him. He
felt it was unseemly, messy, and spoke of preventable failure.
He was always prepared for what he could anticipate and he
planned for the unexpected as best he could. In addition to
the memorized route, he tucked the map into the glove compartment in case of some unforeseen detour. It was hard to
know when he had erred, as he never spoke of it nor directly
expressed frustration or anger. Ever. To shout or swear or bang

his fist was as messy and unseemly as getting lost and pulling over. The only evidence of his distress was the twitching of his clenched jaw muscle. I am sure that, internally and silently, he took himself to task much as his father had. So the memory of his great mistake in Pisa shines out of the past like a flashing beacon, reminding me that even my father was fallible.

My parents took me to Europe in 1965 during the summer of my tenth birthday. It was my first trip there, and the itinerary included Greenland, Amsterdam, Zurich, Mürren, Zermatt, Como, Portofino, Pisa, Florence, Siena, Milan and London. We drove from Como to Pisa in tremendous heat. Travel, let alone driving in Europe, was a challenge for my father. It taxed his meticulous tendencies, as the landmarks of reference were foreign to him.

When we arrived at the hotel in Pisa, we were instructed to park our car some streets away. My father was handed a slip of paper with an address on it and verbal instructions as to how to get there. When we arrived at the designated address, my mother turned to my father and said, "Allen, this doesn't look right." My father was silent because he had the piece of paper with the address and *this* was the place. Before us on a residential street was a building with two tall, wooden, arched doors that opened into a darkened interior.

"Allen, this cannot be right!"

Despite my mother's concern, my father proceeded to drive very slowly into the dark space. The narrow opening did not strike my father as unusual, as he was used to this with our own garage in San Francisco. It even looked similar with its two large blue doors that parted in the middle and but a half inch to spare on either side. He enjoyed the challenge of skillfully maneuvering the car without scratching it. The car inched into the dark, cavernous space. We were all silent. From the back seat I saw stairs off to my right and what looked like a large white box. So intent on the side-to-side maneuvering into the tight space, my father hadn't thought to turn on the headlights.

Finally my mother, staring straight ahead anxiously, said, "Allen, why don't you turn on the lights?"

No sooner were they on than my mother commanded, "Allen, stop! There's a Persian rug!"

And now with the lights on, we all saw the large, colorful Persian rug on the floor, as well as a bureau and some framed pictures on the walls. The white box off to the side was a refrigerator, and now a woman came flying down the staircase screaming, "Esci da casa mia!" (Get out of my house!)

My mother was angry with my father; my father was silent; I held my breath. From the back seat I saw his clenched jaw as he backed the car out of the angry woman's house as slowly as he had driven it in. It felt like an eternity. We finally cleared the tall wooden doors, and the angry woman, still yelling, shut them from the inside with a resounding thud. Behind us a crowd had gathered in the street, watching and laughing.

We drove back to the hotel in a mixed climate of amusement and grim silence. The concierge with only minimal apology said it had been the right number but the wrong street.

In the log that my father kept to mark notable events, the entry for this day reads, "August 12, 1965—Pisa. The celebrated parking incident." It made me laugh to see the shorthand. For years after the event my mother teased him about it; for the longest time my father would ignore her levity. Finally as an adult I challenged him.

"Daddy, it was actually very funny. You are still letting your father command your life. Give it up. It's funny. For all you know, he might have laughed too."

My father was clearly amused by my words, but all he said, with only the slightest of smiles, was, "You might be right."

poker

I TURNED TEN IN ITALY. MY FATHER DID NOT LIKE THE FACT
that I was becoming an age that was a two-digit number and
that my life would likely never involve more digits. He spoke
of wanting to turn the clocks back. It was hard to know how
serious he was in his lament. It seemed grim.

He said this to me in Portofino. We stayed at the Hotel
Splendido, a magnificent hotel perched over the Mediterranean. Our room had a small curved wrought-iron balcony
with a table and two chairs. The waves below pounded the
rocky shore. I remember eating prosciutto and melon. The
waiter ground fresh black pepper on top. It was so delicious
and the balmy breezes so pleasant.

The day my father spoke of two-digit numbers, he also told

me that because I was turning ten, it was time for me to learn how to play poker.

Why, I thought, but didn't ask.

We went out on the balcony with a deck of cards and a box of wooden matches in lieu of coins.

I can only remember the feeling of being perched far out over the sea. Looking down at the coast through the wrought-iron rails, the waves breaking against the cliff. There was not much room on the balcony. I felt the spray from the sea. Exciting. Precarious. Tense. My father's calm voice. I remember the terms my father taught me: five-card draw, seven-card stud, straight flush. The feeling of something important happening that I would never forget.

IN MY FATHER'S LOG I find the reference:

> To Portofino and the Hotel Splendido.
> The wonderful balcony
> Muscat grapes
> Poker
> 8/7/65

I don't recall the Muscat grapes. I can't find a photo of the hotel that looks familiar. The calmness of the Mediterranean depicted on the website does not match my memory of the waves ravaging the rocky coast. The balconies look larger and protected. The wrought iron is not curved.

dogfight

THE HOUSE I GREW UP IN BORDERED THE PRESIDIO IN SAN Francisco, offering a wonderful venue to walk my dog. With views of the San Francisco Bay and Alcatraz, our walks along the dirt paths through the groves of eucalyptus and spruce and the fields of wildflowers were very happy times. Monty always wagged his tail excitedly, sniffed the air hungrily and chased after tennis balls we threw for him. The paths were of endless interest to him with their scents of other dogs, an occasional rabbit or cat. My father and I went together on these walks. When my father reached for his fedora, his coat and the leash from the hall closet, Monty began to dance excitedly on the parquet floors, as eager as I to leave the house, go down sixty-three steps to the street, turn left for two blocks and then take a right onto Arguello Boulevard into the Presidio. Exiting the bustling city, within minutes we were in a world of trees and fields. I asked lots of questions about things that we saw; we talked about the songs of birds, the color of the Monarch butterflies, the spots on ladybugs, the smell of eucalyptus, why moss grew on the north side of the trees but not the south. My father diligently answered all my questions and it made me feel lucky and protected that he knew so much. Several times when Alcatraz came into view, we talked about serious things like what a maximum-security prison was and about the great escape that had taken place in 1962 when I was seven.

On a Sunday afternoon in December 1966, my father and I were along our usual walk. I was eleven. We were talking about Alcatraz. I was preoccupied with the prisoners who had not been found. I asked my father whether the men who escaped might be hiding in the Presidio. He reassured me that this was unlikely, that they probably had drowned trying to reach Angel Island. I felt troubled that he wasn't certain.

Perhaps because this was on my mind, I was startled when on our way back home a man with a hat, a cane and a small mongrel dog at his heels came out from behind a clump of trees. Both dogs were off their leashes. Monty stood still at our heels with ears alert. My father grabbed his collar, clearly assuming the other man would do the same. But when the mangy mongrel lunged forward, Monty broke away from my father's grip and hurled himself into battle.

What followed is stored in my memory as a kaleidoscope of images and sensations twisting and turning in my mind.

My father ran toward the dogs to stop the fight, and the man started hitting him on his back with his cane. I can still hear the raspy voice of the man shouting, "Leave them alone. Let them fight." My legs became weak as I was overcome with fear that I would lose my father and my dog. I slipped down onto my knees in the grass, crying inconsolably, desperately. I couldn't speak.

I have no memory of how long the fight lasted. Probably only a few minutes. When it was over, Monty had a bleeding ear and my father was shaken up but unharmed. As we walked home, I held my father's hand tightly and my father kept Monty on a close leash. I asked many, many questions about what had happened. I don't remember his answers.

In my father's log:

Sunday, December 11, 1966

> *The day of the fighting dogs, the sobbing child. Monty's ear is bitten. The crazy, promiscuous violence that is everywhere can occur in an instant, with as little warning as a dogfight. How little time for laughter, for innocence of the knowledge of violence, and of the death that lies in wait.*

caped devil

EACH DAY AFTER WALKING ME TO THE BUS STOP, MY FATHER
returned home with Monty and then spent the rest of the
morning reading, writing, playing tennis and running
errands. We ate dinner every night at 6:30, served typically by
Yvonne, a French cook from the Bretagne region who came in
the afternoons to prepare the evening meal. After dinner my
father returned to his office and my mother to hers. I went
to my room to do homework. It was not uncommon for my
father to play music in his office after dinner. Not infrequently
it was Mahler. It was always loud, and the deep crescendos of
timpani would often rattle the arched windows of the main
floor of our house. My mother was irritated by the combination of the noise and the fact that my father was in his office

alone, writing rather than being with her. In response she retreated to her office upstairs, shutting the three-inch-thick oak door with considerable force and a resounding thud. With both my parents sequestered in their respective offices, I felt alone and unsettled by the palpable tension.

Though forbidden during the day to enter the living room while my father was seeing patients, I felt I had the right to go into the room at night. Or maybe it was because I didn't think either of my parents would notice, between the music and the closed oak door to my mother's office. Nonetheless, holding my breath, I came down the central curved staircase, careful to avoid the creaky spots in the stairs. I unlatched the small brass hook that fastened the two large glass-paneled pocket doors that closed off the living room from the rest of the house. It was a beautiful room that we used mostly when we had guests or on holidays. A large, fine Yomut rug covered much of the darkly stained parquet floor. A couch covered in warm blue silk velvet stood in front of the east arched window, a rosewood coffee table in front of it. Two smaller dark blue wool-covered couches and mid-century Danish wood chairs punctuated the spaces toward the east side where there was a fireplace. An Austrian silver box with cigarettes, a blue and white East Asian plate, the statues in the windows, the art on the walls. Everything beautiful and in its place.

Standing there above my father's office and under the molded, beamed, twelve-foot-tall ceiling of the living room just under my mother's office made me feel secure. The tension in the house and the fact that the room was somewhat forbidden territory intensified my emotional state of keen alertness. I stood there motionless, yearning to understand what was happening in my father's office. What was he doing? I decided that in the small locked closet of his office he kept a long black cape, which on such tormented occasions he wore. He had to because it was the only way he could exorcise the demons that claimed his soul. I wondered if he looked different as he listened to Mahler and swirled around his office in the billowing folds of the cape.

I was six when I came up with this notion. When I was ten, I noticed the door to the locked closet was open one day. There was no cape—only a large file cabinet and tennis rackets.

In 1999, when I was forty-four, my father was asked to give the plenary address for the American Psychoanalytic Association's winter meeting and I was asked to write a piece about it for the association newsletter. I wrote about the cape and my childhood understanding of his guilty self-criticism as an ongoing battle with the devil. I sent a copy to my father before I submitted it to make sure he approved. He called me immediately. He was impressed and proud. He told me he didn't know I could write so well. And that he felt so understood and so loved. Then he asked with a chuckle, "Did you really believe I wore a black velvet cape to exorcise my demons?"

"Of course not, Daddy, just literary license."

He laughed as I invoked the same defense he often used when challenged about fact or fiction.

blue angels

TWICE A YEAR THE BLUE ANGELS FLEW OVER SAN FRANCISCO. Over the Presidio and Pacific Heights where I lived. Right over the house—six of them ripping up the sky—leaving blue and yellow traces, the roar and piercing crack rattling the windows of my home. It seemed that I was always walking out of the house with my father when they flew over. When I was little, the sound terrified me, seeming to come from nowhere and everywhere. I moved in closer to my father and clutched his hand tighter. I think my father always liked this gesture—a clear demonstration of my vulnerability and instinctive desire for his protection. My hand was small and sweaty, and his, large and dry. We would stop walking as though a great procession were passing before us, blocking our way. My father would often take such occasions to teach me something about the experience—a lesson that would begin in the pause at the doorstep in a moment between feeling scared and protected. I hung on his every word, parsed with deliberate distinction and diction. Over the years I learned all about F/A-18 Hornets, Mach speed, breaking the sound barrier, afterburners, g-forces. One day when I was a teenager the shearing sound above led my father to say with passionate satisfaction: "That is the sound of power." I felt a thrill linking the sounds of the jets with the warm surge of adrenaline spreading within. Subsequently I developed a fantasy of falling in love with a Blue Angel pilot. The fantasy began with the thunderous roar of engines and an exquisite landing. The air hot, and wind blowing every which way. A tall pilot in a blue jumpsuit running toward me across the tarmac: he's smiling, and then I am in his arms, sinking into his powerful embrace.

The last time my father and I saw the Blue Angels fly over the house was a few months before he died. This time my hand protected him. He had terrible back pain and often felt weak and unsteady on his feet; he gripped my hand, knowing I would lend him my strength so he wouldn't fall. We were standing in the warm sun outside the front door when the Blue Angels flew overhead. His movements were slow and the jets were gone by the time his gaze had turned up.

"Ah, I missed them," he said wistfully.

"Daddy, do you have another story to tell me about the Blue Angels?"

"No. I think I have told you everything I know about them."

I felt disappointed. I counted on my father to tell me stories. We started down the street, slowly. I moved closer to him to support him more securely. After a few blocks he said, "Well, I guess I do have another story to tell."

"I knew you would!"

"I heard a story the other day that stuck with me. From an astronaut. He was talking about 'three degrees.' Unfamiliar with that expression, I asked him what he meant. He told me that it is the difference between life and death when he brings the shuttle home. The angle of attack—the angle at which the shuttle is piloted toward Earth. It's exactly forty degrees. Forty-two is too steep and the shuttle gets too hot. Thirty-eight is too shallow; it skips off the atmosphere and the tail falls off. Either way it's over. Even forty degrees is scary but beautiful because the orbiter is bathed in a seven-thousand-degree plasma fireball, which you can see glowing outside each window. Only those infamous tiles stand between you and extinction. Dazzling but dangerous slice of sky in which to fly. Three degrees."

He stopped speaking and his hand felt cold in mine. I felt mildly irritated by the grim existential undertones.

"Are you trying to say that within those three degrees is where we should try to live our lives?" I asked.

My father turned toward me, taking off his sunglasses to see me more clearly. He chuckled and I knew that he was amused by my psychological challenge.

"Maybe if we can . . . when we are able and lucky and ready . . ."

And with that he gripped my arm with uncustomary strength and said, "With you at my side I am ready to walk home in those three degrees."

easter

AS I REMEMBER IT, EASTER ALWAYS FELL ON A BEAUTIFUL
sunny day in San Francisco. The garden was full of life. The
Japanese plum had already shed the last delicate white blossoms, revealing its dense purplish leaves. Beside it was a circular planted area. It was once a fishpond, but my mother had
it filled in and planted a Japanese maple with finely chiseled
pale green leaves and delicate red stems. Begonias, fuchsias
and columbines filled the planter at its base. The camellia was
blooming and the thorny bougainvillea climbing up the side of
the house was full of signs of the paper-thin magenta flowers
to come. Primroses, clematis, and Icelandic poppies rose from
the low concrete planters that ran the length of the house
from the wrought-iron gate to the backyard. A Meyer lemon

and a fragrant pink and white rose planted in large pots stood tall near the front door, and many other pots sprouted white cyclamen and other bulbs. It was a voluptuous garden full of places to hide Easter eggs.

I have been told that for a couple of years when I was a small child my father dressed up in a one-piece bunny suit. I had my eye out for it when I cleaned out the basement after my parents had both died, but I never did find it. Somehow the thought of my six-foot-three-inch-tall, thin, proper father parading as a rabbit never seemed credible. Without the costume or a single photograph as proof, I wonder if the story was apocryphal, made up and then held out as amusing and wishful testimony that my father had such frivolity in him. What I do remember is that my mother scattered dark chocolate eggs and bunnies under leaves and flowers, and my father went to great lengths to hide presents, one for each guest, carefully wrapped, labeled for its intended recipient and hidden cleverly low and high throughout the garden. With choruses of "warmer, warmer, colder, cold, warm, warmer, hot," children and adults were all coached to the discovery of their gifts. The search for presents, chocolate eggs and rabbits required lots of bending over, peering under bushes and lifting up leaves. My mother was always attentive to ensuring fairness, coaching the little children to find eggs and attempting to curb the greediness of the older ones. And then there was always the worry that some of the chocolate eggs would go to waste undiscovered in the garden.

The combination of sunshine, flowers and the reflective colorful foil sparking throughout the garden was festive and pleasing. For many years Monty seemed both intrigued and perplexed by the behavior of the humans on Easter in the garden and in his backyard. One year I noticed him with his nose in the flower bed wagging his tail wildly. When he emerged from beneath the leaves, I could tell he had something in his mouth by the telltale gentle tension in his jowls.

"Monty, come here!" I called somewhat urgently, fearful that he had found something alive. Triumphantly he opened his mouth and dropped a perfectly intact foil-wrapped Easter egg into my palm. One of his most endearing traits was that he had a clear moral sense of what was for him and what belonged to the humans. Food, even inches from his nose, would never be eaten if it wasn't offered to him or placed in his bowl on the floor. And in true retriever style, whatever was in his mouth that he fetched was gently held, as a matter of pride, so as not to damage the recovered prize. By the time I had fully comprehended that my dog had just discovered the art of finding Easter eggs, he was off into the garden looking for more. He got to be so good at it that we had to keep him inside to let the little children find some. He sat by the window with his ears pricked, looking out longingly as the search went on. After the children felt satisfied they had found them all, I dropped one or two of my own into the bushes and then let Monty out. Invariably he found the ones I had left and often a few more.

I live on the East Coast now, where Easter typically falls on a cold day still too close to the grip of winter to feel like spring. Sometimes the vertical leaves of tulips and hyacinths are up, but apart from that the landscape is barren, with virtually nothing else green in which to hide anything. Over the years when we didn't go to San Francisco for the holiday, I did my best for my young son, hiding the foil eggs behind the trunks of trees or nestled into the base of the emerging foliage of the bulbs. The tangle of branches and dried leaves of the honeysuckle or wisteria left over from the fall could at times hide a wrapped present. Bundled up in the wintry garden, I longed for the warmth and sunshine of my childhood.

I bring a small basket with a green ribbon full of dark chocolate eggs and bunnies to my son, now in college in New York. I want to tell him the stories again, describe how his Jewish Viennese great-grandparents loved Easter, how Monty found the eggs. But I don't. Some things are best left in the past. In memory. Or unknown and unresolved. Like the bunny suit.

loss

MY MOTHER LANDED AT ELLIS ISLAND ON SEPTEMBER 13, 1938. She was twenty-two. Her visa had been issued on the first of August after she was asked to withdraw from her medical school studies in Vienna. She surrendered her Austrian passport and was told she could never return. She left Vienna sometime in August, traveled to London and boarded the S.S. *Veendam* in Southampton, England, on September 3. She arrived in New York with a trunk containing some china, linens, clothes, important papers, journals, and jewelry. The rest of her family's belongings were packed up in a carton and ultimately made their way to Denmark, where my mother's uncle Josef resided. Many things were lost or stolen. My mother never dwelled on it. It had been wartime and one was to be grateful for what one had.

MY MOTHER STRUGGLED for years to raise money and procure visas to help her parents leave Austria. Making contact became increasingly challenging and ultimately futile. Letters written by her parents were held up by the Nazis, opened, read, numbered, delayed—some even arriving after the war was over. After they were already dead.

Once when I was six, helping my mother set the table for a dinner party, I sensed her agitation as she opened the locked chest containing her mother's Austrian silverware. The smell of the unfinished wood on the inside of the opened chest and the linen cloth over the uppermost drawer of silver reminded her of home. I asked questions about the little spoons, and whether her parents had had dinner parties too and used the same knives and forks I was laying out on the table. Tears tumbled down her cheeks and she hugged me silently.

"What's the matter, Mummy?"

"You are too young to understand. I'll tell you when you are older."

I heard that answer for many years before I finally learned what had happened.

Her anxiety and distress were palpable. It made me fearful. I didn't understand, nor could I imagine what it might be that I didn't understand. I learned things in bits and pieces.

The information seemed fragile and elusive. I worried that it would slip out of memory.

Now and then on a Sunday afternoon my mother and I would sit together with an album or a box of old photographs. My mother was the only child to her father, Richard, an obstetrician and her mother, Sofie, who had been a nurse in World War I. She played the piano, and once Richard had been an extra in *Aida*. They had two dachshunds and vacationed in Yugoslavia on Lake Bled in the summertime. Little by little she painted a picture of their life and hers. Even more slowly came the painful stories. My grandmother became delusional and obsessed with a well-known composer, tried to kill herself several times and was hospitalized for two years when my mother was four. I learned that my grandfather had a stroke, and it left him with a minor speech impediment, which worsened when he was emotionally affected. While being interviewed by the Americans in 1938, he couldn't speak and they deemed him unable to function in the U.S. workforce. My grandmother was cleared to come to the United States, but she wouldn't leave without him. And then the terrible incomprehensible reality of their deaths. My mother couldn't remember the date and often remarked that she, who never lost anything, had lost their death certificates. After my mother died, I found all the things that she had made reference to over my life. I found boxes in the most inaccessible reaches of her office. They were tied with string and contained all the letters from her parents in their envelopes, carbon copies of hundreds of efforts seeking information and money to acquire visas. I found my grandfather's journal kept while in the bunkers in World War I, my grandmother's journal chronicling her descent into madness, legal documents, medical school records of my mother and her father, letters from family members and friends looking for one another after the war. And among all those things a letter from a cousin decades after the end of the war with a document listing the names of my grandparents as passengers on a train bound for the Polish death camp Sobibor, on June 14, 1942. Upon arrival they were killed in the gas chambers, thrown into mass graves, and burned. Their deaths were never recorded.

All that survived the ravages of war were some of their belongings and my mother to pass along their stories and point out who is smiling in the photo at Lake Bled and the subtle asymmetry of her mother's eyes, which my son and I share. But my mother couldn't bring herself to reel in their past. She left it out in deep water on a slack line. She didn't want to be any closer to her guilt, to the overwhelming trauma and chaos, to the loss. Their legacy lies within me now and in all their letters and journals waiting for my attention. Pages and pages, some over one hundred years old. They will need to be translated. Will I have time to sort it all out before I die? The paper is already fragile, the photographs fading. The weight of more loss pulls at me.

fire 2

I WAKE UP WITH A START, DISORIENTED, TRYING TO FOCUS IN the darkness of early morning and reorient myself to where I am. I have been traveling. Back and forth, Cambridge to San Francisco, to attend to the unwieldy details of my mother's death and the rippling effects of now being an orphan. The loss of the intangible is vast and I find that I hang on to the *things*. I don't want to throw anything away. But I must. And I should. I have so much richness within. So many memories. Layers and layers. But I have become obsessive and ritualistic. I can't give away my parents' clothes unless I can give them to someone I know. I can't alter a stack of letters or photos until I have figured out why they were grouped in that particular way and tied with a silver ribbon. I have boxes of leather-bound classics in German that were part of my grandparents' library in Vienna. I call the Goethe Institute, the German department at Harvard. No one wants the books. I can't put them on the street for the recycling truck. My grandparents were picked up off the street in Vienna and sent to their death in Poland. The parallel is upsetting, so the books stay in boxes in my basement. With everything else that has traveled in time though two world wars and then back and forth across America. I fret about these things. I ordered two large fire safes, and before I travel I make sure to lock up the papers that seem most important. I am constantly thinking, if there were a fire in my house, how long would it take for my alarm system to alert the fire station, four blocks away, to send the fire engine to put out the fire? I consider the time of day, the traffic, how the fire might start.

the dove

MY FATHER DIED JUNE 14, 2007, A FEW MONTHS SHY OF HIS ninety-second birthday. He died in a fashion that would have suited his sensibilities. For years before his death he suffered from back pain. He tried any number of painkillers, which worked for a while, intermittently, or not at all. No surgeon wanted to operate because of his age until he developed sciatic pain in addition to the stenosis in his spine. The pain was so excruciating that he required a walker to go even a few steps, and my father was deeply upset with this harbinger of advancing decrepitude. But ultimately he implored the surgeon to reconsider. Whatever he said to the surgeon must have ignited his compassion sufficiently to offset the obvious risk, for he agreed to operate. My father chose to be awake for the surgery. The two-hour procedure was a success and my father was reportedly very pleased to receive the news. He was closed up, rolled over and ready to go to the recovery room when a large blood clot to his lungs took his life. Even with a full code, he could not be brought back. My mother called to tell me while I was dictating a clinical case, the moment indelibly fixed in my mind. A practicing psychiatrist and psychoanalyst myself, I was sitting in my office in Harvard Square, looking out over the rooftops. When I got off the phone with my mother, I returned to my dictation and then saw a patient. I hadn't expected him to die for a while and nor had he nor anyone else. My mother had made panna cotta for his welcome home dinner. And he was still seeing patients and had appointments scheduled for the week following his surgery. It didn't really bother me that I hadn't said goodbye. It wasn't necessary. Enough had been said. And what wasn't said was already known.

Six months after my father died, my husband left. My son, in the throes of an adolescent bid for freedom, was rarely home and, when he was, he had little interest in my company. With all the men in my life gone, I felt bereft without my familiar bearings and daily routines. Letting myself fall asleep was a challenge every night. I crawled into bed reluctantly, as late as possible, settling into a narrow channel on one side of the bed I had shared for twenty years with my husband. I slept up against a life-size stuffed dog. It offered some comfort to be held in place in the big bed. Books and magazines piled up on the other side like a dam. I never wanted to turn out the light. I didn't want to end the day and I didn't want to become part of the darkness. Each night fell like a cement wall collapsing, twilight racing into the rubble of blackness. Most nights I fell asleep with a book or newspaper on my chest and the lone shaded lamp arcing out from the wall emanating its light and warmth over me. I didn't want to invite sleep by turning off the light in preparation. I didn't want to think or feel or face my dreams. It was less jarring to drift into sleep unwittingly. Even so I would wake frequently in the night with dreams of fire and devastation. And sometimes images of my father's cold, damp face in death, or the sound of his faint voice. Desperate not to lose contact with the voice, I strained to follow it out of my sleep. Sometimes I sat up in bed like a dolphin leaping out of the water, shouting, "Daddy, wait! Don't go!" When full consciousness returned and I remembered that my father was dead and my husband gone, I fell back in bed clutching the stuffed dog. My nights awake became longer and longer as I tried to avoid the tormented sleep. I cried every night and my ribs ached from the exertion of sorrow.

One night in April, I woke up at three to something different. The sky, still inky black, was full of sound. Initially I thought it was inside the house and decided it was the copper heating pipes chirping with the first call for heat. The sound, however, did not fit the intermittent clanging expansion of water pipes. It was an orchestra of sound. After a few minutes of lying in bed listening to the curious noise outside, I pulled off the bedcovers and walked to the window. As soon as I had opened the window, it became apparent that the sound belonged to birds. Lots of birds singing in a pitch black night. A smile spread automatically across my cheeks. I hurriedly put on slippers and a coat over my nightgown and went outside. The night was still, and the air cool. I searched in vain to see the birds. I could tell there were many, maybe a hundred, as their sound was so dense. I stood in my garden in disbelief. Why were these birds singing at three in the morning? The thought made me laugh. What was *I* doing at three in the morning? Spontaneously I called out, "Daddy?" The birds were suddenly quiet. I waited expectantly for a single bird to respond, but within a minute they were all singing again. I returned to my bed. Just as the black night was pulling away from the morning light, the birds stopped singing.

For weeks the birds sang in the night. Always a chorus of chirping. During the day I occasionally asked my neighbors what they thought of the nightly visits of the singing birds, but no one had heard them. In the midst of my sleep-deprived state and my growing doubt about my mental functioning, I wondered if my grasp on reality was slipping away. I never saw the birds or even determined where they were perched when they sang. I never heard them fly away. They provided solace nonetheless, punctuating my fragmented sleep with their playful chatter.

On June 14, 2008, exactly one year after my father died, the birds did not sing. The coincidence was disturbing and I stayed up all night hoping the birds would return. The next night the birds didn't come either. It made me feel as though I had lost yet something else. I had let myself cater to the fantasy that my father was one of those chipper birds, singing because he was now out of pain. I wanted some signal to tell me that he was still out there. The following night, desperately tired from two sleepless nights, I finally sank into a restful sleep. I awoke at five in the morning, immediately upset that I might have slept through the birds' visit. I dressed and went outside. Day was just starting to break and the sky was thick in mist. I sat down on the cedar love seat in the garden. It was cold and damp. From nearby came the muted flutter of wings. I struggled to locate it in the mist but couldn't. There was only silence.

I felt disheartened. I started to rise to go inside, glancing upward. To my surprise, perched on the telephone wire above my head was a lone dove. It was a large bird, its head pulled down as if cold and trying to stay warm. It seemed tired and didn't move.

"Daddy?"

In the blink of my eye and as a tear dampened my cheek, the dove was gone. Neither the singing birds nor the dove have returned since. But then again, I can now turn off the light.

the office

ONE OF THE FIRST THINGS I DID AFTER MY FATHER DIED WAS to go to his office to get his appointment book so I could contact his patients. My mother sent me with the keys. "Come right back!" she said, reluctant to let me go alone.

The office was peaceful and uncluttered. I sat in his large black leather chair—something I had never done while he was alive—and took in the view as he had known it. The two beautiful Oriental rugs lay on the rich mahogany parquet floor. At the far side of the room stood a wooden desk that he had had built; it spanned the entirety of the wall and had multiple drawers and cabinets with shelves beneath. A large blotter in a leather frame lay at the midpoint of the desk in front of the high-backed office chair. The desk held a pair of black-framed reading glasses, a netsuke of a monkey and a small ruby red cut-glass vase from Austria with two sharpened pencils, a Parker ballpoint pen and a maroon Montblanc fountain pen. A silver and gold dish full of beach stones made by a local jeweler, Victor Reiss, lay atop a small wooden box with multiple drawers. My mother had it made and engraved for their second anniversary in 1957. Above it a small barred window faced the outside steps. It had a straw shade that allowed light in but was opaque from the outside.

From his consulting chair my father could discern who was approaching the front door. He would know by the time of day and the outline of the person and their movement whether it was the garbage man or the deliveryman from Swan Oyster Depot or me coming home from school. Large teak stereo speakers sat on the desk on either side of the window, and a small fine antique Baluchistan rug hung on the wall. A green marble chessboard awaited the next move. A framed copy of Munch's *Dance of Life* leaned up against the wall, along with a picture of my mother in 1938 with her parents at a train station. The mahogany-paneled wall behind his consulting chair was bare but for a hanging glass lamp. A few feet in front of him sat the patient's brown leather chair and ottoman. Sometimes I sat in that chair when my father summoned me down after dinner for a serious talk. The analytic couch was separated from his chair by a Danish teak credenza. On its one shelf sat his stereo receiver along with a photograph of my mother smiling. On top was a black glass paperweight with a design

of waves and a moon, the maroon S. T. Dupont fountain pen I
had given him a few years before he died, two ballpoint pens
(one red), a sharpened pencil, and his current appointment
book. I imagined him the night before his surgery. Leaving his
office for the last time. Did that thought cross his mind?

To the left of where he sat was a custom-built rosewood
bookcase and at eye level an entire shelf of black appointment books lined up chronologically. The shelf below had
CDs—the ones he played most often: the Mahler sympho-
nies, Schubert impromptus, Beethoven sonatas. His diction-
ary, his own books and some of his current or favorite books
(*On Heroes and Tombs, Under the Volcano, Light Years, The Engineer of Human Souls, A Heart So White*) were on the shelf above.
Several more shelves above were also full of books. Nietzsche,
Popper, Camus. The bookcase ran to the edge of a large three-
paned window that looked out over a large planter box with
shrubs and trees growing from it. A white filigree curtain let
in light and the shadows of the trees and bushes while main-
taining privacy from passersby climbing the stairs to the front
entrance. Beneath the windows was a low built-in rosewood
bookcase; a handblown glass candle holder in the shape of a
mermaid, a green ceramic bowl and various other treasures
sat on top. Underneath, two bookshelves with *The Columbia Encyclopedia*, stacks of the *TLS* and the *New York Review of
Books*. The patient lying on the couch faced a wall of nonfic-
tion books, and the other walls of bookcases contained the
fiction all alphabetically organized. At the foot of the couch

was a Danish wooden chair upholstered in white leather with a blanket and a patchwork velvet pillow my father's mother had made for him. One narrow, locked wooden door led to a closet, which held a three-drawer filing cabinet with patient records and other important documents. On either side were his tennis rackets, spare lightbulbs, rags, and padded envelopes for mailing books. A small heater was mounted in the wall.

The air was chilly. I got up and turned on the wall heater as I knew my father always did when he entered the office. I didn't want to leave. Furtively I unlocked his desk drawer. Any minute my mother would be calling down through the elevator shaft for me to hurry up. My heart was pounding and I felt clammy. I opened the top drawer. There was his worn manila folder of postage stamps, each denomination of stamp separated by a sheet of waxed paper from one cent on up. I remember coming down to his office at night to ask for a stamp and he would take out this folder. "What would you like?"

"It's a first-class letter."

He would let me pick—maybe a six-cent stamp of an American bald eagle and a two-cent Cape Hatteras or a six-cent stamp of the landing of the Pilgrims and two one-cent songbirds. I loved to watch his fingers carefully passing the pages so I could see and choose. He always used beautiful stamps, and when I left home for college we each selected stamps for the letters that we sent each other. A love stamp or one of California or just something particularly beautiful. I started to keep my own collection of stamps and would be pleased when I discovered a new special-issue stamp before he did.

My mother called for me from upstairs. Feverishly I took the stamp folder out of the drawer before locking it. And then I returned to his chair and took the maroon-colored pen I had given him. I put them under my sweater. I felt greedy. I was alone in the forbidden office where, until this very moment, I had only visited in my father's presence. I felt guilty yet entitled to be there. I unlocked the next drawer. In it a large box taped shut and labeled "Private, Do Not Invade. Journals" and beneath it a locked metal box. The gun box. I'd forgotten all about the gun, but seeing the box recalled the story.

When I was five, my father bought a Smith & Wesson Model 19, .357 magnum, with a four-inch barrel, from Abercrombie & Fitch. My mother was very opposed to guns generally, let alone one in the house. She insisted that the dangers of having a gun were far worse than the dangers of not. She was most worried that *I* would find a loaded gun. But my father decided it made sense to have a gun on hand to protect his family in case of an unforeseen menace. He had a door with a lock and key made for his open-shelved night table. He kept the revolver inside in a gray steel cash box that had a keyed lock as well. Some of the bullets were kept in a box inside the bedside cabinet and some in his desk in his office. I'm sure my father imagined the scene that would lead to his firing the gun and rehearsed it in his mind repeatedly. He wakes up to the sound of glass breaking downstairs as the intruder enters the house. He sits up in bed, reaches for his keys to open the bedside cabinet, then unlocks the cash box, takes out the gun, then the bullets, loads six, stands up, and unlocks the bedroom door. There my father, in his pajamas, faces the marauder and fires. His family is safe, nothing is stolen, and the criminal is shot but not killed. The police arrive, handcuff the intruder, and commend my father for his heroic behavior.

After a few years the gun was moved to a locked drawer in my father's office. The reason became known only years later when my mother told me that she prevailed on my father to move it out of the bedroom. I can only imagine that she described a different scenario than the one my father had been envisioning. My father wakes up to the sound of breaking glass. Disoriented, he slowly becomes aware that someone is in the house. He sits up, fumbles for his keys. He opens the bedside cabinet, takes the gun box out, fumbles again with the small keys to unlock the box. As he takes out the revolver and loads it, the bedroom door is broken down by the criminal, who is unarmed. He sees the gun, grabs it and points it at my father. The practical realities of using the gun eclipsed the notion of the John Wayne hero he might have hoped to be.

The discovery of the journals and the gun rattled me. As I heard my mother coming down in the elevator, I shut the drawer and locked it, replaced the stamp folder in the top drawer, and put the pen back on the teak bureau. I grabbed the appointment book and left. No sooner had I locked the office door than I remembered I had left the heat on. Struggling with the keys, I got back into the office and turned off the heat just as my mother appeared from the elevator. She was agitated.

"What are you doing in there?"

"Nothing."

"Give me the keys!"

My mother entered the office and looked around. "I don't like being here. Let's go. We'll deal with this office another day." We never did.

She gave the gun to my half-brother, let me take the pen and told me that the taped box of journals was left to me. She added that I couldn't take them yet as she might want to read them. The stamps stayed in the drawer, and I was never alone again in the office until after my mother died.

thoughts

From Allen to Ilse
19 April 1997
43rd anniversary

THOUGHTS

I

He thought

I had a treasure
but somehow I lost it

The birds fly north
I'm sad

II

He thought

I had an ordinary thing
but thought it a treasure
It doesn't matter
I lost it

The west wind is cold
I'm disillusioned

III

He thought

The real illusion
(if that makes any sense)
is to believe in treasure at all

The leaves fall
I'm cynical

IV

He thought

> I have lost everything
> the stoicism to stand unmoving
> in the blistering desert
> The hope to stumble on
> after the glimmering blue water
>
> The trees are bare
> I'm desolate

V

He thought

> what is this thing?
> slipping through my fingers
> glittering in the moonlight
> beckoning dancing
> teasing entrancing
> quicksilvering through my fingers
> so fast so fast

I'll cup my hands to hold it

In the dark wood the trillium is blooming

I'm happy

fire 3

WHEN I WAS NINE YEARS OLD, THE HOUSE TO THE EAST OF ours in San Francisco caught fire. Unlike most of the houses in my neighborhood, this one was not contiguous with ours but perhaps twenty feet away, and because we were on a hill sloping downward, it sat lower than ours. I can't remember what day or time this occurred, but I was home, and my father was in his office. My mother called into the elevator shaft for my father to come. There was something urgent in her voice. An unfamiliar siren of danger in her tone. I ran downstairs. I heard the elevator coming up. The front door was open, and I saw the flames next door. I heard and saw the glass of the windows shattering and smoke billowing out. There was a terrible smell. My mother was standing outside holding full-sized pillows from her bed. I was more frightened by the sight of my mother with the pillows than by the fire.

"What are you doing with the pillows, Mummy?"

Her expression was one I had never seen before. I was relieved to hear the elevator door open. My father came out as my mother answered my question: "We might have to sleep on the street tonight."

I didn't know how to understand that; it was such a foreign and unfathomable notion. My father put his arm around my mother. "Ilse, we won't be on the street."

"The house could explode."

"No. It will be okay. The fire trucks are just around the corner."

We all stood there. My mother a foot shorter than my father, nestled in his arm, still holding the pillows. I don't know for how long. I remember asking my mother why she thought we would have to sleep on the street. She was cross with me as though I was poking fun at her.

"You don't know what I went through. What it was like to go through the war."

"And you still haven't told me what happened to your parents!" I retorted in my defense.

"You are still too young."

When my father died, his body was *managed* by the Neptune Society. His wishes were for the simplest inexpensive disposal of his remains. No embalming, no wake, no funeral. A cardboard box and cremation. Perhaps because there were not the typical events to organize the acceptance of the deceased, attending the cremation became important. But we weren't prepared for what this would entail.

The crematorium was in Emeryville in the East Bay. Industrial neighborhood. A long flat-roofed metal building with a blue door and no windows. Three short, wide smokestacks were billowing smoke. A small sign to the right of the door with the words "Families Ring Bell." Inside was a small waiting area with pale green walls, artificial flowers and a few uncomfortable chairs. We were then escorted to an inner room where the cremation occurred. Very clean, sterile machine room. Metal and concrete. Nowhere to sit. Two or three ovens with temperature gauges and signs "Danger Hot." My father's body lay in a covered cardboard box. The attendant asked if we wanted to see the body. My mother, always slightly suspicious of the nefarious motives of others, wanted to make sure it was my father in the box and I felt the need to accompany my father all the way to ash. The table at the height of the oven was lowered so that my mother could see in and the cardboard top pulled back. There were droplets on my father's face. Like sweat. Like there was still life. It made me feel cold and breathless. Except for that fluid lysing out of the skin cells, his face looked more sunken and lifeless, his features distorted by the ravage of decay from within. It seemed clear that most families probably did not opt to be present in this room for the cremation. Conversation with the attendant was awkward. He spoke of the temperature at which the body is burned, between 1400 and 1800 degrees Fahrenheit, and how important it is to sweep everything out of the chamber. He showed us the special brush to reach into the corners. And then he asked if we wanted the bone fragments left with the ashes or taken out. I wondered why one would want them out. My mother said to keep everything. He added that sometimes families didn't want anything that wasn't ash because it was disturbing.

The lid of the box was repositioned and the table was raised again to the height of the topmost oven. The box was slid into the oven on mechanical rollers. A vertical metal door then lowered, blocking the box from our view. The attendant told us we could go to the other side and watch though the small round window. Fiery orange flames, corrugated innards of the cardboard box, a glimpse of my father's skull stripped of hair and skin. When I stepped back from the little window, I saw my mother sink into the protective arm of my tall half-brother. It reminded me of the day when the house caught fire in San Francisco. She had the same look in her face from forty-four years before when I still did not understand. Shattering glass, Kristallnacht, my mother's parents being burned by the Nazis. And now the love of her life on fire before her eyes.

the last letter

IN *THE LISTENER* (1999) MY FATHER WROTE:

. . . All marriages are unhappy. None of my friends and none of my patients has a happy marriage. An unhappy marriage is the normal state, not a deviation. The unfortunate reaction, therefore, is to feel bitter about it, to nurture grievance, to imagine that married to someone else one *would* be happy; for this reaction leads one into actions and attitudes that make an unhappy marriage *more* unhappy, rather than into those responses which would tend to make an unhappy marriage less unhappy.

The main reason for misery in your marriage (I'm still talking to myself) is your tendency to think that you're entitled to a happy marriage, that with a little luck you would have had it. You must accept the given unhappiness as normal, and proceed immediately to do whatever you can to diminish that unhappiness. What you have is the human lot. (p. 164)

No doubt these lines were a source of many conversations between my parents, conversations I didn't hear. Yet I witnessed the ravages of strain in their faces and the retreat to their respective offices. Among their papers I found this letter, written in the blue-black ink of my father's Montblanc fountain pen on the occasion of my mother's birthday.

October 11, 2000
Dear Ilse,

  Eighty-five and a summing up. Now or perhaps never.

  But first, one last effort to clear away the dense thicket of misunderstanding that has grown up about my now infamous leitmotiv: All marriages are unhappy.

  For anyone haunted by the image of a union that is perfect because the love is unconditional, all intimate relationships are unhappy simply by falling short of that ideal; and the vision of life issuing from that discrepancy is dark. Such is the case perhaps only for a few; I choose, as a literary device, to say <u>all</u> because that irrational extension of the personal becomes an outcry, suggests a failure so grave as to be disorienting, and thereby conveys the drama and the pain of a doomed quest.

But why, you might ask, do I honor an unattainable yearning?
Is that not the elevation of neurosis into a guiding principle? Yes
exactly. And why might I want to do that? Because, at a time
when I was still <u>entitled</u> to a little, I was not permitted to <u>ask</u>
for anything.

("Why did you come in the house, son?"
"Mama said dinner was ready."
"Did you ask <u>her</u> if dinner was ready?"
"Yes, sir."
"You trifling, no account scoundrel! Get yourself back out in that
yard and cut grass till she <u>calls</u> you to dinner. You understand?"
"Yes, sir.")

And long after the forbidding voice was silenced, its prohibition
sounded within, preventing me from all asking—from standing
before an audience, for example, thereby <u>asking</u> for recognition.

But as I surrendered my right to <u>ask</u>, I found a fierce privacy
within which I defended my right to <u>want</u>. From the ensuing
battle for my soul, neurosis, the sick defender, emerged as the
tattered victor. If I am not allowed to <u>ask</u> for anything then I
will seize the right secretly to <u>want</u> everything, including the
unattainable ideal.

That was the wanting that enabled me to find you, and to
recognize in you that which I sought, and the marriage we created
is an ongoing celebration, a perpetual feast; for in you I found
someone who gave without being asked, gave prodigally—lavish,
exotic, glittering emotional gifts such as I would never have known
how to even ask for. Our conflicts generated profound joys—as,

indeed from the beginning, you assured me they would: "That you were once unkind befriends me now."

The vast polarity of our natures, making for so much contention, has yielded enormous benefits. I, an American, because of you, have become a world citizen. Our *goyem* are better, but their art is richer, their thought more complex, challenging. Within European culture I found my intellectual and literary home. Even among the Americans it is the expatriates like Eliot rather than the homebodies like Whitman with whom I feel the greater affinity. Because of you I have relocated my origins.

And I, so averse to travel, because of your pushing and pulling and persistence, have entered into airplanes, and have deplaned from them in strange lands, and so have actually seen those places whence my spiritual legacy has come. What I live by has thereby acquired a reality not otherwise obtainable. I can, in San Francisco, read that "Nietzsche spent summers in the Swiss Alps," but to walk through his cramped ascetic rooms in Sils yields an importantly different kind of knowing.

And I have found in you a nobility that derives from your disposition to love others, not for what they may then offer you, but for their own sakes; and this trait in you has become for me a faith that sustains a high secret self that otherwise would long ago have been lost to cynicism.

And this greatness of soul appeals not only to me but also to everyone who has the tact and patience and sensibility to find it in you—for you don't wear it on your sleeve!—and these people then value you, become your friends, gather around you, and since

I'm with you they become my friends too, and by them too my life
is enhanced.

And I found in you a playfulness and passion potential in me but
throttled by an ascetic renunciatory solemnity, whereas in you this
quality, at the first notes of a waltz, bursts forth in a gay, sensuous,
sexy dance. So you become the probate court to deliver to me my
belated legacy of passionate life.

And now I see that what began as an accounting, a balance sheet
of profit and loss and intimacy, has become a love letter. So be it. I
admit it. I affirm it. I declare it. I love you.

Allen

My father died seven years later and my mother carried
on for another four years, stoically taking care of his estate
in probate, continuing her psychiatric practice, surviving a
bad fall with a hip and wrist fracture at the age of ninety-
four. With reluctance she stopped her psychiatric practice at
age ninety-five. When I asked her, "Why now, Mummy?" she
replied, "I don't want to become one of those dwindling clini-
cians. I want to go out when I am strong!" I went to see her for
Christmas 2011. She knew she didn't have much time left. Par-
kinson's and a couple of old indolent cancers were ultimately
getting the better of her, slowly sapping energy and strength.
She ate little and spoke slowly. My last conversation with her
was at the kitchen table. We sat across from one another. She
asked about my life. I encouraged her to eat. After she had been
quiet for a long time, I asked, "What are you thinking about,

Mummy?" She looked up at me but was silent. I felt dread that the opportunity to speak to my mother had receded out of reach. But finally she responded, "I was thinking about making love with your father."

Two weeks later, on January 9, 2012, on a sunny day in bed, my mother was listening to Schubert. She was smiling, clapping her hands together and then just slipped away. There was no food in the refrigerator. There were no patients to cancel. She left everything in order.

last rites

MY PARENTS CAME TO CAMBRIDGE TO VISIT ME EACH SPRING
and fall—two seasons, dramatic in their intensity, that were
different from what they knew in San Francisco and reminded
them of their beginnings together in Stockbridge, Massachusetts. They especially loved walking in the Mount Auburn
Cemetery. It was an occasion for my mother to celebrate life
captivated by the spectacular shows of spring blossoms or fall
color and an opportunity for my father to contemplate death
(or "our shabby end" as he often called it) and the ultimate
gloomy meaninglessness of life. These walks allowed for the
predictable and charming intersection of their differences.

"Allen, it's so beautiful here. I think we should consider
being buried here. What do you think?"

"If that's what you want, that's fine with me."

"But Allen, what do *you* want?"

"Well, I don't really care."

"Well, you have to care! You need to have an opinion!"

"I want to be with you so wherever you want to be will be fine with me."

"But what do you want as an individual?"

"I don't care."

"How can you not care?"

"Because it doesn't matter."

"Well, it matters to me."

"Well, if it were left up to me I would want to be buried in the orchard in Puget Sound."

"But it's so isolated there. No one will come visit us."

"I like that."

"And furthermore, you are so silent and brooding. I will feel lonely."

"Well, like I said, whatever you want will be fine with me."

"At least if we are buried *here* there will be a lot of interesting people for me to talk to."

"Okay, that's fine."

IN THE END my father did lay claim to his wishes. In *The Life and Death of My Mother*, published in 1992, he wrote:

When I die I want my body to be cremated, the ashes buried in the orchard on the island in Puget Sound, the site marked by a flat stone of green marble bearing my name and dates, and, a small distance below, my paradox.

How to live?
Who knows the question knows not how,
Who knows not the question cannot tell.

Those three lines sum me up: the inquiry that has driven me, and the impasse into which it has invariably delivered me.

I choose the orchard because there, among those gnarled and broken apple trees, blossoming unseen on the empty air, dropping their wormy and unwanted fruit for the deer and the crows, the loamy land sloping down to the slough, the blue heron standing motionless on one long spindly leg, mirrored in the still water, the steely blue Sound beyond, and far away on the horizon with jagged Olympic Mountains, icy, snow-covered, distant—there, at times, I've had a sense of home.

Actually I would prefer to be buried there, my body intact, in a plain cedar box. But that's hard to arrange; and, as between lying intact among strangers in the cemetery or lying in ashes and bone fragments in that magical place, I choose the latter.

And I can see it coming about. Soon. I shall not have long to wait. And when it's done, my wishes all exactly met by a loving and respectful family, it will gratify me not at all; for the consciousness that now wills it and is capable of gratification by it shall have vanished. Indeed, it would matter not to me, at that time, were my body thrown into the garbage. I am carefully arranging something that cannot possibly become a reality until its purpose and fulfillment have become unknowable to me. So any brooding on that site, any ghostly gratification, must be claimed in advance. Now.

So . . . this is the future scene to which I suppose I am now laying claim. A late summer afternoon, the sun disappearing behind the Olympics, the sawtooth ridge knifelike against a pale green sky, clouds red and gold, becoming pink turning to gray turning to black. Far far overhead, silently, the plane passes, leaving a glittering silver trail. A sloop with a blue sail glides past the beach. The heron rises ponderously from the slough, the great wings beating slowly, heavily, uttering his hoarse and protesting cry. From the table at the edge of the cliff near the house come voices, the sounds of dinner—my children and grandchildren, friends, dogs. Joan wanders alone down to the twilit orchard, glances at the green stone, reads again the pithy anguish of my life. I always wanted to write in stone: now I will have done so. She directs towards me a current of melancholy affection, reexperiences the quite special bond between us. This stone is partly covered by the long dry grass of autumn. I must clear that away, she thinks . . . plant some flow-

ers. Perhaps tomorrow. She glances . . . and passes on . . .
and that's all. (pp. 24–26)

When my father died, I did find a piece of flat green marble
and had his name and dates and his paradox carved into it. We
placed the stone in the orchard and my mother read the lines
above. But my mother didn't put his ashes in the ground. They
stayed with her in San Francisco in a wooden box in a blue bag
on a dresser in my parents' bedroom. After my mother died,
I took both boxes of ashes to Puget Sound. And yet I couldn't
put them in the ground either. It felt uncomfortably perma-
nent and inaccessible. And I had too many questions. Do I
mix the ashes and bury them in one hole? Do I leave the ashes
in the plastic bags? How deep shall I dig the hole? What do I
do with the wooden boxes with their names engraved after I
remove the bags of ashes?

In what used to be their bedroom, the two blue bags sit
on an old oak dresser. That the question still exists as to what
to do with their remains comforts me. The presence of such
opportunity somehow keeps their lives intact. I can imagine
taking them back east again and burying them in the Mount
Auburn Cemetery where my mother would have more company. But for now they are together in that beautiful place.
My father is where he wanted to be: with my mother. I don't
think he is silent and brooding. I imagine they have plenty to
talk about.

the log

IN 1990 MY FATHER GAVE MY MOTHER AS A BIRTHDAY PRESENT
a one-hundred-page document entitled "PARTNERS, A log
of the Journey 1951–." It begins a few months before my father
met my mother. The entries are pithy in outline form:

> 1951, January—Deeply depressed
> July—Ilse arrives in Stockbridge

Some are evocative allusions to their romantic beginnings.

> October 7—Sunday   I deliver a carton of grapefruit to
> Ilse who now lives at an apartment on Main Street.
> December 30—Sunday   The long gray afternoon

One hundred pages of entries: who came to dinner parties, what meetings were attended, doctors' appointments, comings and goings, births and deaths, annotations on the meaningful and the mundane. My mother showed it to me. Amazed, I asked my father how he could possibly remember all of this. He told me that in his appointment books he wrote such notes down in red ink. Of course he had kept all of these appointment books—thirty-nine of them by 1990. He went through them all and collected his entries and made the log. For my mother, now for me: a reference book to anchor my discoveries of their journey and mine.

the audograph

AFTER MY MOTHER DIED, THERE WAS A DELAY IN FACING THE
"dungeon," as the main storage area of our basement had
affectionately been called all my life. The space lay under
the kitchen and dining room and abutted the landing where
patients either went directly into my father's office or took the
elevator up to my mother's office on the top floor of our house.
Accessible from the kitchen and down a flight of steps, the
dungeon was midway down the basement corridor that led
to another door through which was the landing. The entrance
to the dungeon was two feet off the floor of the basement and
had a flat wood door and padlock (which was never locked
although always in place). The door opened out 180 degrees
when fully extended, but if you didn't open the door fully, it

could slam shut, locking you in with no escape. I suppose this is how the space came to be called the dungeon. The keep of our castle. The enclosed area was four feet high with exposed plumbing pipes. At the far end was a small latticed sash three feet off the floor of the dungeon but six feet above the floor of the landing on the other side. Once between patients my father needed something from the dungeon and accidentally locked himself in. Peering out from behind the sash he called out to my mother's next patient, who was about to enter the elevator. She was disoriented and confused to hear my father's voice and then startled to see his face appear from the darkened space above her. As the story was told over the years the patient was then instructed to proceed down the basement hall to release my six-foot-three father from the locked dungeon.

The dungeon was an archeological marvel with its layers of history buried in boxes and bags and suitcases. It was also the place where extra rolls of paper towels, tin foil, toilet paper and boxes of Kleenex were kept (and my mother always forgot that they were there) along with old clothes, books, toys, unwanted gifts, papers and financial records—out of the way of the elegant quarters above but kept here as testimony to the long, rich, full lives of my parents.

One of the first things to be sent to Goodwill after my mother died was my parents' Audograph, a heavy gray machine that could record and play floppy cobalt blue discs. No sooner had it been removed from the dungeon than I came upon a stack of these discs in envelopes that had been mailed across the country between my parents. I checked the dates, January and February 1954, and knew these likely were love letters sent before my father left Stockbridge for San Francisco to marry my mother. My mother, married to her first husband, Ernest, and living in California, had gone to the Austen Riggs Center in Stockbridge, Massachusetts, in 1951 to complete her psychiatric residency at the urging of her psychoanalyst, Erik Erikson. My father, married with two small children, was on staff there, having followed his psychoanalyst, Robert Knight, from the Menninger Clinic in Topeka a few years before my mother arrived. Unhappy in their marriages, my parents began an affair soon after my mother arrived in Stockbridge in 1951. They fell in love, but by the time my mother returned to San Francisco two years later, they had said goodbye, having forsaken the idea of being with one another. That was August 1953. In December they attended the psychoanalytic meetings in New York. In my father's log the entry on December 6 reads, "The decision is made." They knew then that they could not bear to remain apart.

I called the Goodwill on Clement Street where we had taken the Audograph, but it was a fool's errand, as they had no idea what I was talking about. "I'm looking for an Audograph, which I brought in last week."

"Whose autograph?"

"No, Audograph. It's a heavy gray machine, the precursor to the tape recorder."

"A tape recorder? We have several."

"No, it's not a tape recorder. It's *like* a tape recorder but big and heavy. It's gray and plays cobalt blue vinyl discs."

"Oh no, we don't have anything like that. Call the main office."

Several phone calls later I was no closer to finding my parents' Audograph and sadly acknowledged the possibility that I might never be able to listen to the blue vinyl discs. I found information online, and upon the suggestion of my sister-in-law I started looking on eBay. Almost two years later, two Audographs were posted for sale: $50 to buy the two and $50 to ship. The machines looked familiar, sending an arrow of memory back from childhood when I made my debut at age three with a recital of "This is the house that Jack built." I recalled staring at the large gray machine with the white light on, holding the microphone and becoming out of breath as I got to the end of my performance. It seemed a questionable purchase as only one turned on and neither functioned. When I brought them to my friend Bruce, an electrical engineer, he too looked dubiously at the machines. "I'll do what I can. You'll need to give me some time though."

"No problem."

My mother had died two years before and those discs had sat around for fifty-six years before that. I could wait. In fact, knowing that it was a possibility made me a bit hesitant, even reluctant to listen at all. A friend had commented to me that I should throw them all away—that it was their life, not mine.

Then again, they could have thrown it all away themselves or if they couldn't bear to do that, could have left a note saying "Please do not listen, destroy upon my death." But neither had done so.

When Bruce called a month later, I expected to hear that his efforts to revive the antique machines had failed. But to my surprise he said, "I just heard your father tell your mother how much he loved her and how he couldn't wait to see her."

AND SO BEGAN my journey into my parents' passionate and tormented love life. Each day I transcribed two new discs—a daily visit with my parents, their voices so familiar—speaking to one another before I was born. They spoke of their great and deep love and desire to have a baby, but also their anxieties and guilt about breaking up two marriages, leaving two children on the opposite coast, getting divorced.

Each of my parents had kept the letters and discs of the other in their office files. My father's communications to my mother were bound in loose ribbons and placed in unlabeled boxes; my mother's correspondence to my father was neatly organized in labeled folders. When I opened my father's file labeled "Letters from Ilse December 1953, January and February 1954," the first thing I found was a small slip of paper with the words "Audograph machine is in teak cabinet in dungeon." Was that in case *he* forgot? Or was he ensuring that I could find the machine and listen to these tapes after he was gone?

I was a much-wanted child and loved deeply by two extraordinary parents. They gave me much in their long lives and then left me with their treasures and secrets: the letters and journals, photographs, official documents and correspondence of my parents, grandparents and great-grandparents. Against the odds of a century of time, several continents and oceans, two world wars, divorces and so many moves by boat, rail, plane and car, it is miraculously all with me in my house in Cambridge.

string of all sizes

IT WASN'T UNTIL MY MOTHER DIED ON JANUARY 9, 2012, THAT I went through my father's office and packed it up. He was meticulous and maintained his papers with unique and impeccable care. When I was a child, he told a story about the discovery of a box of string after the death of a ninety-five-year-old angler. He had a wooden box with six small drawers that sat on his desk. The drawers had labels to indicate the length of string in each drawer: String 24–36 inches, String 18–24 inches, String 12–18 inches, String 6–12 inches. In each drawer there were several pieces of each length of string tied in gasket coils. In addition to a drawer labeled "Tools" that contained several pairs of scissors in different sizes, there was another drawer labeled String Too Short to Use. My father was amused by this story for the obvious parody of his own obsessive tendencies taken to a new extreme.

Outside of his writing, my father was a very private man and all but two drawers in his office were kept locked. My mother also was very private, and after he died, she took the office keys and hid them along with all the other keys that were most important (the key to the safe deposit box at the bank, the skeleton key to the chest of silver). It would be a major event when we would take the house elevator down to his office to find something she needed. The office was always chilly, and I think my mother wanted my presence to steady her anxiety about entering my father's shrine. As soon as the checks or a health insurance form or the like was located, the drawer would be locked up and the keys returned to their secret hiding place.

When my mother died, I had the keys and access to every-thing. The known, the secret, the forgotten pieces of string of all sizes.

love

MY FATHER LOVED ME DEEPLY BUT NEVER SAID SO DIRECTLY
until I was twenty. It was 1975 and I was a junior at Harvard
College and had been sick. My parents returned from France
where they had been vacationing to help me navigate abdomi-
nal surgery and a brush with cancer. I had multiple postop-
erative complications and my father stayed for several days
after I had returned to my dorm. I was weak but determined
to return to my college life. My memories are thin as I felt
exhausted, the challenges of each day eroding the strength of
memory. I recall that the day before my father left to return
to San Francisco, he washed my long hair. Unable to be fully
in the shower, I sat on the floor of the bathroom in his hotel
room at the Sheraton Commander with my head over the tub.

It was a tender moment, almost too intimate. I felt the familiar certainty of the care and attention of my exacting father. The day he left, in suit, tie and hat as always, I felt an aching pain of impending loss. I think he did too. As the cab pulled up on Walker Street outside my dorm, he turned toward me, stretching his long arms around me, pulling my body gently toward him. Without looking at me, he whispered, "I love you very much."

Without pause I said, "I love you too." I wanted the moment to stand still as much as I wanted to break away from his embrace. It felt almost too much to take. Typically my father was so silent and his presence so formidable that I often felt fearful that I might upset or, worse, alienate him. I always worried that I had to be careful around him, that any misstep might incur his wrath or his retreat. These thoughts were in my mind as he drove off—this time it was I who stood in the road, waving my long arm as he waved from the back seat of the cab. Within a minute he was out of view.

Three years later I was reminded of this event. It was August of 1978. My father came into my room in our summer house in Puget Sound. He sat down next to me and handed me a large bound book for which he had fashioned a beautiful book cover out of fine Italian wrapping paper. He handed me an unmarked, unsealed envelope. On the outside of the card was a reprint of Claude Monet's *Poplars* and on the inside, in the blue-black ink of his gold-capped black Parker fountain pen, he had carefully written:

Dear Joan—

This is the story I have been working on during the last several years, another version of The Tragical History of Doctor Faustus. *I am not sure it is finished, but it is dedicated to you and already, finished or not, belongs to you.*

Love,

Daddy

I felt the same tension as I had three years before—a welcome heaviness holding me in place next to my father, sitting beside me on the edge of my bed, and an imperative to spring up and run out of the house, through the orchard and down to the beach, to release the tension in my body.

The manuscript was entitled *The Scheme of Things* and on page 2 were the words "For Joan." Over the next few days I read the manuscript and recognized myself in the character Abby and my father in Abby's uncle Oliver. The story revealed how my love and reverence for animals and the sanctity of life had surprised and moved my father and how it taught him something about love and attachment. Much of the novel was true and what wasn't might as well have been. About some things I am no longer sure.

The novel details the story of my much beloved dog, Monty. When he died in 1975, it was but a few months after my own surgery. I was preoccupied with school and romantic interests and was absent from the goings-on at home in San Francisco. A year earlier on a visit home for Christmas, I had noticed

that Monty seemed awkward on his feet. He was soon diag-
nosed with prostate cancer and had to be euthanized a little
over a year later. My father and I had always spoken of burying his body at our summer home in Puget Sound, but when
it came down to it, my father held him as he died but then
left him at the veterinarian's office. When my parents called
to tell me this news, I immediately said, "What did you do
with his body?" My father, overcome with emotion, got off the
phone and my mother whispered from the other extension,
"Your father is very upset. Don't talk about it." And I didn't.
Not then nor for many years after. And when I thought about
that phone call, it made me feel acutely guilty. The following summer in Puget Sound we found a piece of driftwood
that bore some resemblance to Monty's physical form and we
mounted his name and the years of his life, 1963–1975, upon it
with slender brass numbers and letters. No longer recogniz-
able as a dog, the wood is still there, slowly decomposing, and
the brass letters and numbers are falling away.

In the novel my father tells the story of how Oliver feels
accused by Abby. Wracked by guilt for having left their beloved
dog, Barney, at the vet, he becomes obsessed with finding the
body and ends up at the city dump, digging day after day in
vain. His colleagues worry about his mental health. A year
later, Oliver finally finds the remains of Barney. When I read
this, I felt my heart pounding in a combination of anxiety,
incredulity, guilt and dread. Had my father actually done that?
Did I drive him to it? Driving to the local landfill and dig-

ging for a dead dog? I was away at college. He might have. The question haunted me.

It took almost a year for me to ask. I had graduated college and was living in Berkeley, California, visiting my parents on a Sunday afternoon. My father was sitting with my mother in her office. He was reading Galway Kinnell's *Book of Nightmares*, and my mother was going through her mail. When my mother stepped out of the office to make us tea, I felt a sudden need to know the truth.

"Daddy, I need to ask you something."

"Yes?" he said, peering inquisitively at me over his reading glasses.

"Did you actually go to the dump to look for Monty?" I felt faint as if any moment my legs might give out beneath me. I wanted to know and I dreaded the answer.

My father took off his reading glasses altogether, and with a bemused yet ever so slight look of critical disbelief he replied, "Of course not, sweetie!"

I blushed and turned away. I felt embarrassed and relieved. Reassured and freed of the guilt that I had felt, I then reread the ending of the novel. Oliver has taken the remains of Barney to Puget Sound and dug a grave. He says:

> "Well Barney what can I say to you? Abby is far away.
> When, as a little girl, she would speak on such an occasion I would stand by and listen. I would listen as an adult, sympathetic to an expression of feeling, which,

though heartfelt, I considered childish and sentimental. I was present not to learn but to comfort. I had no sense that she was speaking for me. But she was. She was putting into words something I was learning to feel. So as she has at such ceremonies spoken for me, now in her absence I speak to you for her.

" . . . You're home and it's time to say good-by. From here we go separate ways. You are going down in the earth, there from to become part of the ongoing waves of life. What will happen to your spirit—to that devotion, that radiance in your brown eyes, to that way you had of racing into the wind on a white beach, of leaping high in the air—I don't know. But so long as Abby and I live, all that is safe will live with us." (pp. 191–192)

It made me cry, as it still does each time I go back to it. His words, witness to his deep love, echo back through time, erasing any doubt I ever had.

goodbyes

THE ACCUMULATED EXPERIENCE OF DEPARTURES FROM MY parents is deeply etched in my mind—lugubrious and poignant, agonizing and tender.

My mother rarely went to the airport to see me off but liked to spend time with me and my father before I left the house. Sometimes my departure would result in her giving me some cash or a gift—something important to her from her home in Vienna that she kept in a secret cubbyhole in her office. She prepared a bag of smoked salmon or prosciutto sandwiches, fruit and Florentines from Fantasia bakery for me to take on the flight. My father sat in the leather chair in my room with a book or newspaper and kept me company while I packed.

Frequently my flights were at night and my mother cooked a dinner for us, which we ate in the kitchen. Long before I had to leave, she would start worrying that I would be late. When finally we had to go, my mother hugged me tightly with both anxiety and resignation. She had left Vienna in 1938. She left both parents behind. It was clear that she worried each time I left that she might never see me again, like her parents.

My father always took me to the airport. He accompanied me to the gate. Always early, we sat together until boarding was nearly complete. He embraced me and then positioned himself so he could watch me walk down the ramp to board the plane. I looked back and waved as I passed from his sight. Once I was on the plane, my father moved to the window at the waiting area and, knowing what seat I had, he would try to position himself to maximize the likelihood that I would see him as the plane taxied down the runway. He also memorized the number on the tail so he could tell when my plane had taken off safely. He never left before my departure was certain. Often I did see him from my window seat. A lone, tall figure waving at the window, and sometimes he could see me waving back as well. The protracted goodbyes tethered me in tension like an arrow pulled back, waiting to be released.

As my father grew older, he stopped driving me to the airport and we said goodbye at home. We rode the elevator down together to the garage and walked out to the street where the cab waited. Unaware of the weight of the moment, the cabdriver typically sped off unceremoniously as the door was pulled shut. My father moved to the street and waved, as did I until we lost sight of each other.

My son takes the bus to New York. I pack him things to eat and drive him to the bus station near my house. I park the car and walk with him to the bus. We embrace and gaze tenderly at one other. But for just a moment before he boards and takes a seat. The windows of the bus are dark. He is not burdened by these goodbye rituals. I watch as the bus leaves the station. I wave. He doesn't. I am saluting the past, not the present.

rain

ON WEDNESDAY, SEPTEMBER 24, 2003, MY FATHER WENT TO the DMV to renew his driver's license. He was a month shy of turning eighty-eight. It was typical that he would have planned ahead, in case of any mishap. He went in the morning when he would have otherwise been playing tennis. He failed the eye exam and, due to some idiosyncratic California law, a Supplemental Driving Performance Evaluation was required. The rationale behind the law was to see if the driver's performance behind the wheel could compensate for poor vision. So if my father wanted to renew his license, he would need to take a driving test, which he would have to repeat every two years if he wanted to continue to drive. I can only imagine the ardor with which my father determined to take on the challenge, faced with a beacon of his mortality. After all, he was still playing tennis, driving to and from Golden Gate Park. When he told me he would take driving lessons to prepare for the test, I felt amused, proud and fearful listening to his plans. I felt he shouldn't be driving at his age anyway, even if he could, and at the same time I felt proud to see him so determined to do it.

In his appointment book, starting on October 1, is the chronicling of these lessons: the name of the instructor, the school, and sometimes commentary about the instructor. The first part of each entry is written in red ink, but his description of the teacher follows in pencil, as if he wanted to be able to change his commentary.

October 1, 10:30 am, Ron Moore Driving lesson,
    petty, scolding
October 3, 12 noon, John Li, Lucky Day Driving School,
    indulgent, not good
October 6, 5–7 pm, Thomas, International Driving School
October 7, 9 am, Art McNally, Mission Driving
    School, good
October 8, 9:30 am, Driving instruction, Dragon Driving
    School, not good
October 13, 2–3:30, Neal Goddard, Atlas Driving
    School, the best
October 15, 3:10–5, Ron Moore, not good
October 16, 8:30, Art McNally

I recall his telling me about the different instructors, and that McNally, a retired state trooper, said to him at the last lesson, "You're ready, pop! Good luck!" After eight lessons, on Friday, October 17, six days before his eighty-eighth birthday, the entry is "9:30 DMV driving test." And he passed. The license would be good for two years.

He did continue to play tennis, but it became more difficult. He had an arrythmia and was started on medication that made him dizzy. He took a couple of bad falls. While he didn't break any bones, he was bruised, body and soul. My mother was alarmed and urged him to stop playing. In his appointment book on April 11, 2005, an entry reads, "Joe—?last tennis." Joe had been one of his steady partners for many years and indeed there were no more entries for tennis dates after that.

Prior to his ninetieth birthday he took two more driving lessons and again passed his driving test on Monday, September 26. His driving after this included taking himself and my mother to their doctors' appointments, grocery shopping at Cal Mart and Bryan's Grocery, dinner out at Vivande on Fillmore Street or with friends. Nothing too far and no highways.

On February 7, 2007, I flew by myself to visit my parents. They were both still practicing and my father had just published his thirteenth book. I thought it might be useful for them to have more help at home as they were both more compromised physically and my father had had a bad fall outside the local market. But while they allowed me to arrange a few interviews with candidates, my father was vehemently opposed. He said resolutely, "It's not necessary. And I don't want any strangers in the house." I felt troubled for having upset him, torn between wanting to step in and protect him and respecting his steadfast stubbornness.

I was leaving San Francisco to return to the East Coast on Saturday, February 10. It had been raining all day. The usual cabdrivers my parents made use of were away or otherwise too busy given the weather. Around noon we called a cab company to arrange a pickup at 8:30 for my red-eye flight back to Boston. As had become common, we had dinner together in the kitchen rather than in the dining room. The familiar routines of my parents had slowed down and there was a somber hesitation in our conversation. There was unspoken sadness and anxiety embedded with resigned acceptance that once again I was leaving San Francisco, that I might not see them again. Ever again. Time passed too slowly and not fast enough. We cleaned the kitchen together, my mother packed me a little snack for the plane, and we moved to the living room to wait for the cab. But the cab didn't come. By 8:45 we called again and they said they were delayed but would be coming soon. When it was 9:15 and still no cab, my father said, "I'll take you." It had been years since he had driven me to the airport. It was nighttime and it was pouring rain outside and it was a thirty-minute drive on the freeway.

"I don't think that's a good idea, Daddy." Not wanting him to know that I was worried about his ability to navigate the highway, the rain and the dark, I continued to insist that the cab would arrive soon and that the weather was too terrible. And it was late. My parents were usually in bed at this time. The cab didn't come and at 9:30 I reluctantly agreed to my father's proposed plan. He seemed excited, almost elated as he fetched his hat and coat. Then my mother suddenly decided she would come along too.

I asked my father for the car keys, hoping he would not insist on driving to the airport as well. Without pause or hesitation he handed me his keys. He was smiling. He sat in front with me, and my mother sat in the back seat. The rain was torrential and we drove in tense silence. Yet the car was full of my unarticulated thought: I wished my mother hadn't come because if there was an accident, I might lose both my parents. And I was glad my mother did come because she would keep my father company, keep him awake. If they got back home alive, my father would feel great. If they didn't, he would have been glad to know he had died without cowardice. I had a gripping stomachache by the time we reached the airport. I could hardly bear to part from them. I thought about changing my flight and driving them back home, but I knew none of this would happen. I kissed them goodbye, hugging them as if it would be the last time, and told them, fighting back my tears, that I loved them both very much. My father was tender but matter-of-fact. "You had better go, sweetie, or you'll miss your flight. We'll be fine." With that he got into the driver's seat, my mother at his side, and they drove off. I waved in the rain as they were swallowed up by the stormy night. My flight was delayed and I called the house before taking off. My father answered the phone. "Everything is fine. I feel exhilarated, like a young man again. I didn't think I had it in me anymore. It was great!"

I visited San Francisco again in April a few months later. My father allowed me to drive him around town to do the errands. I was surprised that he let me, but I didn't comment as we made our rounds to the markets, hardware store and post office. At some point he turned to me and said, "After that trip to the airport in that rain, I have nothing more to prove."

was affectionately described as mouse-eaten. There was a lot of talk about how he ought to feel a little sheepish for hacking away at his hair himself, especially in view of the fact that he was a psychiatrist, a psychoanalyst and a well-known writer. But he didn't. And whether he knew that his behavior would ultimately result in my taking on the responsibility, I'll never know, but I suspect that was the case. He never stopped cutting it himself, but when my visits were frequent enough, he would do it less often. When many months had gone by between visits, I felt punished for my absence by the ravaged hairline.

Whether he was asking for a trim or a major cut, I would try to rectify the mouse-eaten edges while chastising and teasing him for his folly. I cut very slowly and small amounts at a time. I moved around him constantly, holding up tufts of hair to compare the respective lengths. From side to side I combed it one way, then another, sending him to the mirror to check how he liked the length. No matter what I did, when I was done he would compliment me on my handiwork. Once when he asked me to cut a little more from the sides, I snipped at the air without actually cutting any more hair. I told him to go check again and he did, announcing that now it was perfect.

The haircut was an excuse to be together, in close physical proximity. We spoke of poetry—Philip Larkin, T. S. Eliot, Rilke, Neruda, Yeats—and he would frequently quote an entire poem from memory. We spoke of the meaning of life, death, and the vicissitudes of self-deception. We spoke about

Nietzsche, Lou Salomé, Kierkegaard, and Popper. When we weren't talking, he would often close his eyes, enjoying the sustained and sanctioned touch of my fingers. I did too.

When I visited in April 2007, my father, then ninety-one, asked for a major cut. When I reminded him that I would be back in July, he admitted that he wanted a different, shorter cut and of even length all over. I was surprised, as he usually preferred a longer, wilder cut. "What do you want to look like?"

Without pause my father answered, "Gary Cooper." We both smiled.

"Okay," I said.

It was a cold April day, and we decided to use the bathroom for the haircut rather than our usual place in the garden. It took a long time to cut his hair, moving around my father, from side to side in the cramped bathroom quarters, cutting and combing. Of course I pretended to know what Gary Cooper's hair looked like. We were both silent.

As my father grew older, I often felt an urgent restlessness, seeking conversation to receive his wisdom and memory, aware that time was running out. "Tell me about the War of the Roses." "What were the names of the plays you directed in the theatre in Austin, Texas?" But on this day I was content to be silent, as was he. Just the shearing sound of scissors. He closed his eyes. He was relaxed and content, his breathing slow. I asked him to look in the mirror a couple of times and each time he did he wanted it shorter. In the end he found it to be just right. And just like Gary Cooper. "I think this may be the best cut ever," he said. The thought crossed my mind that it might be the last. For several years I often thought that when leaving San Francisco. Waving out the back window of the cab as he stood in the street—his long arm arching slowly and deliberately till we lost sight of one another.

But it was not the last time I cut his hair. Getting ready to leave for the funeral home in June 2007, I thought to bring the shears. His hair was flat, damp, combed back, and I felt shocked by the coldness when I went to touch his head. I took the shears from my purse. Like a thief raiding a safe, I pillaged from the haircut I had so painstakingly made but two months before. I felt guilty, looking at the obvious invasion, imagining certain disapproving consternation for my disrespect of the dead. I took a picture with my cell phone. My hands felt stiff and clumsy and my movements furtive, as if any moment someone would enter the room and apprehend me for my egregious transgressions. I reminded myself that I was invoking arbitrary customs for which my father had little patience.

My father hated memorials because he felt they gave legitimacy to the falsification of human nature. Cleaning up the portrait of a life in cloying eulogy was ultimately deceptive. My father would have been content with my telling this story, even somewhat bemused to see his daughter carry the banner he passed off. I expose us both in a tribute to him and to our relationship. Profound but not simple. The underbelly of a great attachment is not without a vital yet uneasy tension of insecurity and certainty, fantasy and denial, exposure and secrecy. I have a silver tuft of my father's hair and a snapshot of him dead, but I have all of him alive within where the secrets of love are secure.

mosquito destroyer

WHEN I WAS IN MY EARLY FORTIES AND MY SON WAS SIX YEARS old, my father sent me a children's book entitled *Papa, Please Get the Moon for Me* by Eric Carle. Though clearly intended to be read to my son, it was not sent to him but to me and was inscribed, "To the little bird from the mosquito destroyer."

My son asked, "Who is the little bird?"

"In the summertime Grandpa used to write his books sitting on the old oak rocking chair with the green leather seat. He liked to sit on the covered deck outside the little study that Grandma had fixed up for him. But one year the swallows had built their nest on the wall of the study under the eaves and Grandpa's presence on the porch was far too close for the mother swallow and she started to dive-bomb him. At lunchtime Grandpa said he was going to take down the nest. I protested. He said little and after lunch moved inside his study. I was so upset that I wrote a note and then I pretended to be Monty. With the note in my mouth I leapt up in front of his window to show with some urgency that I had a note to deliver. He came to the door and I gave him the note. He didn't take down the nest and resigned himself to write inside his study. Thereafter I was nicknamed the little bird."

My father wrote about this in 1999 in his autobiography, *The Listener*:

> Swallows have built a nest under the roof of my porch a few feet from where I sit. With all the places available to them—house, barn, shed, water tower, the whole unpeopled island—they choose the one place I have chosen for my work. And that would be all right with me, I would share quarters with a mother swallow, but it's not all right with her. It makes her nervous for me to be so close. She wants me to leave. Moreover, she has a husband and a lot of friends. All of them are after me. They circle and scold and, one after another, bank and swoop on me as dive-bombers on a battleship, pulling up at the last moment. "The nest has got to go," I say. Joan is shocked, disbelieving. "You wouldn't tear down a nest, Daddy! Not with eggs in it!"
>
> My concentration is lost for the morning. I go for a walk on the beach, thinking I will take it down when she

is occupied with other things. In the afternoon returning to my porch I find the sheet of lined paper pinned to
the rocking chair. On it printed awkwardly in crayon:

Dear Sir,

I know you have work to do, but I'm going to have
babies. Please don't tear down my nest. Sincerely, Bird

I pick up my gear and move inside the cabin, surren-
dering the porch to the swallows. (pp. 148–149)

In a file labeled "Joan," amid school reports and pediatrician
notes and a brief essay I wrote on having my tonsils out at age
five, there is my hand-scribbled note from the bird. As with
the notes and letters from my mother, my father has added the
date in pencil. August 1964. I was nine years old.

"What is the mosquito destroyer?" my son asks.

"Do you remember my room at Grandma and Grandpa's
house? It was at the back of the house. It had a lot of windows
that opened out onto the backyard. It was shady and a little
damp and mosquitoes used to come in the windows. I was
afraid of them not so much because of their bite but of the
noise they make. Actually it wasn't even the noise, it was when
the noise stopped. I would thrash around in bed. Eventually,
I felt very upset and would get out of bed. Monty was upset
too because I was upset and would get up and stand next to
me while I called out for Grandpa. 'Daa-dee, Daa-dee!' After a
while I would hear the key unlocking their bedroom door and
Grandpa would appear at the end of the hall, in pajamas and

his silk robe and a silk bandanna that he wore over his eyes at night. He carried a folded newspaper, as he sleepily made his way down the hall to me. Once in my room, he would turn on all the lights and start searching for the feared enemy. It often took a while to locate and destroy them. Sometimes my father had to climb onto my leather desk chair or get on the desktop to swat the mosquito. Monty would get excited and try to join in the action by following us around. Only after the mosquito or mosquitoes were destroyed by the rolled-up *San Francisco Chronicle* would my father leave. This often went on for days at a time. After a while Grandma and Grandpa bought cheesecloth to cover my bed, but the mosquitoes still seemed to get in and finally they had all the open casement windows replaced with screened ones."

"Why were you so afraid?"

"Because when the buzzing stopped I knew they were biting me but I couldn't see them."

As I tell my son this, I remember that when I was older my mother used to tease both my father and me that this was all about an Oedipal bid for my father's attention. But whatever the unconscious motivation, I always knew that my father was my hero, my mosquito destroyer.

My father wrote about this too in his novel *The Scheme of Things*:

> At night Oliver wakes to a wailing cry, "Daaa-dee! Daaa-dee!" He struggles up out of sleep, out of bed,

economy of motion

OFTEN BEFORE A DINNER PARTY OR FAMILY OCCASION, MY
father would lay a fire in the living room hearth. When he
went to get wine from his cellar, he took down the large basket
and filled it with the seasoned wood that he kept in the garage,
along with pieces of the wooden wine crates to use as kindling. As with wrapping presents, there was a right way to do
it. It never was obsessional, but aggressively precise. The flue
was opened. Two individual sheets of the *San Francisco Chron-*
icle were crumpled up. It was important not to use any more
paper, as it created unwanted ash. Next came small pieces of
wood from the wine crates, then slightly larger pieces of wood
staggered across the smaller ones, and larger logs on the top,
all precisely arranged to allow ideal air flow among the pieces

of wood. It was a matter of pride that the proper placement of two sheets of paper, the right amount of kindling, logs and one match would be sufficient to ignite a robust fire. With a single short match he lit the paper in three places, and then tossed the match into the fire before placing the fire gate in front of the hearth. He never stayed to watch whether it caught. He knew it would. It didn't require anything more, and I certainly never saw my father hovering over tentative flames. He always did it right, and when others offered to help, it made me cringe. Wads of paper, too-large pieces of wood, a flicker of promise and then messy, ashy failure—the attempts at resuscitation by blowing at the dying flames, spewing ash out onto the pale granite hearth and dark parquet floor. My father, though, never said a word at these times, though I suspected that he was critical of these efforts and how they did not obey the principle of "economy of motion."

My father liked things done without any unnecessary movements. He liked the power of precision. He wrote that way—spare yet rich. And he spoke that way—with his love of clarity, finding just the right words parsed with powerful eloquence. There was never any "uhm," "hmm," "gosh," "you know" in his speech. It was orderly and enunciated with precise diction like the crisp conducting of a symphony orchestra. He approached everything like a chess game, traveling forward in time to consider all factors, small or large, that could affect the execution or influence the outcome.

He loved to watch me work in the kitchen. He felt that

my ability to prepare risotto and a rack of lamb and sauté green beans and make a salad dressing and have it all ready at the proper time was the pinnacle of the economy of motion. He sat at the table watching me, describing my actions. "You make it seem so effortless. I see that you have arranged your tasks in your mind and now have things arranged around you in a way that doesn't require you to move around unnecessarily. You are accomplishing so much, yet there is no frenetic motion. It's marvelous to watch."

"Economy of motion?" I teased him. "Right, Daddy?"

"Exactly!"

My father loved that I appreciated this notion too. He taught me how to build a fire, but he never insisted I do it that way. Yet he was so pleased when he saw that I did. Six months before he died, I was visiting in San Francisco with my husband and son, celebrating Christmas. My father had a lot of back pain, and I could tell that he didn't feel like bending over to build a fire. It was chilly in the room and I told him I would build one. Crouched down on the floor, I could feel his eyes on me as I laid paper and pieces of wood. I lit the match, catching the three points of the two pages of the *Chronicle*, threw the match in, stood up, replaced the fire grate and turned to face him. The fire caught and my father caught my eye. He smiled and I returned the smile along with a tilt of my head in deference. He didn't say anything. His smile was fragile and I knew he wasn't feeling well. But I also knew that in this moment as I turned and looked in his face—in that split second that *the log, part 2*

THE LOG MY FATHER MADE FOR MY MOTHER'S SEVENTY-FIFTH
birthday spanned the years 1951 to 1990. He died in 2007, and
when I came home for the cremation, one of the first things I
did was go to his office to get his appointment book so I could
cancel the patients scheduled for the upcoming weeks. In so
doing I saw the entire shelf of black appointment books, lined
up by year. There was no doubt in my mind they would get
packed up, along with everything else from the shelves, in the
locked drawers and in the closet. I had no idea, though, of the
scope and breadth of what I would find.

So now almost ten years later I am in my office in Cambridge with a box full of his appointment books. I could make
another log covering 1990 to 2007, plucking out the details in

red ink and in pencil pertaining to the comings and goings of family, travels, dinners, tennis dates, medical appointments, and any other significant event. Type them up and label them "The Log, Part 2." Do I do that? For what audience? Who cares? Do I really need or want to know? How will I decide? If I don't, will they stay packed until I die and my son comes upon the box? He will think of how often he said to me that I should throw more things away, that I lived too much in the past. He can throw them away. Why can't I? If it is gone, it will no longer be accessible. It's the abandonment of the possibility to know.

After my father died, my mother asked me to take down boxes from the upper shelves of her office closet. Most were filled with photographs. She wanted to tell me what she knew before it was too late. Sometimes together we would write the names or dates down on the backs of the photographs. I noticed once a box labeled "Credit card receipts 1965–1970." "Mummy, you know you don't need to keep this kind of thing for taxes. You only need records for seven years." Her silence was notable. Of course she already knew that. I waited on the chair for further instruction as to what box to bring down. I caught sight of many boxes of credit card receipts. All in five-year increments. I wanted to blurt out, "Let's get rid of these. Please don't leave all this for me to do when you are gone." But I knew it best not to trespass on this order of things anymore.

And soon my mother said, "Bring down those credit card receipts."

"Which years?" I asked mockingly.

"The one you were just looking at." The box was labeled in my father's handwriting. Within it were five years of monthly statements, each with the receipts attached. I marveled at the tidy organization. I handed a year's worth to my mother.

"It's so interesting to see what your father and I spent our money on back then," my mother remarked. "See? We bought the teak dining room table from Danish Imports in 1966. It was expensive. Your father and I debated whether to buy it for a long time. It was around the same time he was buying so much French wine. Here, Connoisseur Wine. See how much he spent on French wine? That was a lot of money then. It's interesting to remember these things."

The thing that reminds you of something that might otherwise be forgotten. But if one doesn't remember it's there, then it falls to chance whether it will be discovered. And does it matter if I don't remember? It exists. I asked feebly if I should throw the box away now that we had a look at it. "No, just put it back!" I knew the next time it would come down would be after my mother died when I would then remember looking at it with her. And these thoughts. The thing that activates the reclamation of memory, the rich layering of time and experience. Built like a stone wall. Each rock carefully examined, rotated, and fitted into place. And then it is no longer the individual rock. It is part of the wall. The wall stands. We can always go back and look for a particular rock. But will we find it? Remember where to look? And then one day the wall will fall away too.

So will I make "The Log, Part 2"? Maybe I'll learn something I didn't know, or maybe something I don't want to know. The trail of crumbs through the woods. The birds eating the crumbs. The witch waiting.

hospital bed. Her eyes were closed. Her lips were parted. Her hair was combed back. There was a sheet folded neatly across her chest. She was wearing her favorite nightgown. Her hands were resting on the outside of the sheet. She wore her wedding ring and her favorite green jade ring on her ring finger. Impulsively I lowered the rail and lay down beside her. She was stiff to the touch, with just a hint of warmth in her body. "Oh, Mummy," I called out. I didn't know what to do.

Mona came up and told me how peaceful her death had been. "She was listening to a Schubert impromptu, clapping her hands. The windows were open. It was unusually sunny and warm for January. She thought you were here so she let go."

It was four in the afternoon. "Shall we call the funeral home?" Mona asked.

"No, not yet," I answered without really knowing what I had in mind. I felt disoriented. I went into her office and sat in her chair. I looked at all the books and sculptures, boxes and lamps, so familiar to me for so many years. I stood up and looked for the skeleton key she kept under the rug by the elevator door. It was comforting that it was still there. I unlocked her inner office, formally a dressing room and bathroom but converted by use into more storage space for financial files, patient records, boxes of photographs, presents, clothes. It was a place I was forbidden to go by myself. Now I stood inside. Rolls of wrapping paper stood in the bathtub, and there were boxes of Christmas cards and ribbons from the Christmas just past. I found a small piece of a log of dark chocolate–covered marzipan wrapped in red foil and a partially consumed box of Calissons d'Aix. She kept such goodies there so she could have a little something sweet to eat between patients without running to the kitchen. I remembered that my mother would at times offer me one, at most two calissons, so that they would last a long time. These almond candies brought to my mother by friends who had been traveling in France were coveted and rare. I ate them all and the marzipan too. I then went to her analytic couch and pulled off the two mattresses and dragged them into her bedroom. I had dinner with Mona and her mother. I don't remember what we ate or what we talked about. I spoke with my family. Arrangements were being made for them to come. I was exhausted. I got ready for bed and lay down on the mattresses next to my mother. I decided her spirit might leave her body while I was there and I could have a farewell with her as she wanted.

"Good night, Mummy," I whispered into the darkness. "I love you."

I sank into a deep sleep, and when morning came I opened my eyes, hoping for a signal that her spirit was present. I wanted to see a bird fly through the window, or hear the call of a dove in the garden. But there was nothing. I got up and dressed and took the two rings off her finger and put them on my own. I called the funeral home.

"When did your mother die?"

"Yesterday. January twelfth at one-thirty p.m."

"Yesterday?"

"Yes."

"Why did you wait so long? It's standard to call within a few hours of death."

I felt angry at this intrusion.

"Well, my mother wasn't in any hurry to leave her house." For that matter, *nor* was I in any hurry to have her go.

Within an hour the black-suited men had arrived from the funeral home. My mother was put in a body bag and placed upright in the elevator. She rode down to the garage for the last time.

stored in the basement in a large Market Street Van & Storage box with a logo of a cat carrying a kitten. A smaller lidless box contained the strings of white lights and stockings along with colored lights and gaudy metallic balls at the bottom, which were never used but for whatever reason stayed in the box. I never asked about them; I can only imagine my father brought them when he moved to California to be with my mother. Maybe they had been from his mother.

Whatever family and guests had congregated took part in the ritual of decorating the tree. First came the strings of white lights, which had been painstakingly placed back in their boxes from the year before—each light fitted precisely into a separate slot in a plastic tray with the wires collecting in a trough in the middle and slid back into the fraying cardboard boxes. My father would be the one typically to string the lights, the rest of us giving advice as to the placement and spacing. After the lights came the handblown clear glass balls. Twelve of them in a box, each with a loop of twine of different length so as to have maximal flexibility for placement. My mother was forever reminding us to be careful lest they break and to position them so that they would catch and reflect the white light. At the top of the tree my father secured a golden angel with a pipe cleaner around her waist. It was a charming figure cut from an olive oil can with metal shears by my mother's first husband. It always seemed touching and odd that my father adorned the tree each year with his predecessor's handiwork. Then came a variety of ornaments, many from Denmark made of wood or cornhusks. There were thin painted red wooden hearts and gingerbread people. There was a hand-blown glass hummingbird and an angel made of feathers, a metal rocking horse, and a colorful hand-painted silk fish. Each ornament was wrapped in tissue paper and packed in a box labeled by my mother as "Best Ornaments" or "Very Best Ornaments." We took turns placing them on the tree. As the years went by, my mother began to voice her preference for decorating with the white lights and glass balls only. She said she found it more elegant, but I think decades of the cumulative fatigue of packing and unpacking ornaments became tiresome to her. I found it comforting to open the boxes with the same tissue paper around each special ornament year after year. I never missed a Christmas in San Francisco with my parents, and typically I was the one to insist that this ritual should stay the same.

After the tree was decorated, we attached our stockings with thumbtacks to the edge of the mantel over the hearth, though not without debate initiated by my mother about how the grown-ups really shouldn't have stockings. My father's sister, June, made my stocking—red velvet lined with green satin with my name and a decorated Christmas tree made of sequins. I was three when she gave it to me and was breathless with pleasure when I saw it.

With the stockings hung, we then proceeded to fetch from various quarters of the house our presents, which were not from Santa Claus and not for children, and placed them under the tree. When all was done, we left the room, closing the large glass pocket doors behind us to make our way to our respective beds. As soon as my son and his cousins were tucked in, several of us crept back to the living room, unlatched the living room doors, took down the stockings and began filling them. A concerted effort with multiple Santa Clauses. My mother always put Satsuma oranges at the bottom of each stocking, along with dark chocolates and a few small gifts. My sister-in-law came with large bags of gifts, each thoughtfully selected for a particular person, which filled the stockings and often overflowed onto the hearth. Hilarity ensued between the whispering so as not to wake those really waiting for Santa Claus and the intermittent "Don't look!" to one another as we placed some item in, on or under a stocking intended for someone standing three feet away. Then the presents for the kids were placed under the tree, usually accompanied by my mother's concern that there were too many presents, that the children would be spoiled and expect too much and so on. Sometimes my mother remembered she had forgotten something and would take off to her office to find it. It was lively and chaotic. My father typically excused himself from all the commotion to read in bed.

Christmas morning was never organized around the habits of children. While my father never said anything about it, I think he felt that Christmas was a good opportunity to offer lessons in restraint. Nothing happened before nine except the mounting restlessness of children. My father presided over breakfast—grinding coffee, making fresh orange juice, heating pastries, cooking bacon, setting the table. At some point my father agreed to opening the stockings as we drank our coffee and then returning to the presents under the tree after breakfast. As an adult, I was typically in charge of the orange juice, squeezing twenty to thirty oranges. When finally we had finished breakfast, then the dishes had to be put away. It was often eleven before we all sat down to open presents.

Given the revered tradition for using beautiful wrapping paper, opening presents became a spectacle of waiting and watching. It was not deemed proper to open more than one present at a time. The card needed to be read out loud as there might be a witty or poetic clue at which to guess. The ribbon and Scotch tape were meticulously taken off the package and then the present opened and passed around for all to see. Not everyone gave allegiance to this ritual. Sometimes the card was overlooked and the paper ripped off, making my mother wince. Discussions about beautiful paper and cards, about the meaningfulness of being together as a family, were common. Those who tended to rip open the packages received inexpensive paper from the five-and-dime with stick-on gift tags the next year.

Christmas morning often extended well into the afternoon because whenever my mother had to go to the kitchen to do something for dinner we had to pause. It was not uncommon that it would be three o'clock before we were done.

With the years came new protests about our rituals. One

year my mother said, "If you see the same wrapping paper three years in a row, then it can be thrown away." Another year it was decided that unless you were a grandchild of my father, you would not receive a present. Attempts to limit presents or the amount of time allowed to open a present were considered. Once an attempt was made to have only stocking gifts so we could have more time to go out for our Christmas walk. I protested all change, liking it just the way it was.

After my mother died, the two boxes of ornaments were shipped from San Francisco to Cambridge in the spring of 2012. Like everything that came from my parents' home in San Francisco, it was comforting and jarring to see it in my house. Comforting because the things provided shortcuts into memories of my parents and jarring because their existence in my memories belonged to another place and time. I didn't want to open the boxes. I was afraid I would let the genie out of the bottle, that something would be lost and that the loss would be final. They were shabby and weak. It felt unreal to see the now sixty-year-old box with the logo of the cat carrying the kitten in *my* living room. The smell of the basement in San Francisco lingered as I opened the box, and an overwhelming sense of time as both flimsy and solid swept over me.

Attentive to the order in which the smaller boxes were packed into them, I begin to unpack the two boxes. Hesitantly. I am by myself. I feel the eyes of my parents watching me as they always did. They are sitting on the couch, *their* blue silk velvet couch. With each string of lights and each ornament I place upon the tree, I untether it from the past. By the time the boxes of best ornaments are empty and I am climbing a ladder with the angel, I feel that tying her to the top of the tree will complete the transfer, like data from an old computer to a new one. Teetering on the top of the ladder, I tighten the pipe cleaner around the angel's waist and the highest vertical bough, draping a few inches of lights to dance off the golden figure. I feel warm; as if the combined and vast energy of all the Christmases I had known were passing through me and beyond like the ripples of gravitational waves reaching out from space. I turn to the blue couch. My parents are fading from view, their features blurred as they depart the moment. I climb down from the ladder. I stand back. The tree is beautiful. I feel wistful. And energized. Different from before. I decide to find new boxes for the ornaments and lights. I take a picture of the cat carrying the kitten on the old moving box in case I become nostalgic. I then break down the boxes and carry them outside for recycling. It is a moonless cold night; the sky twinkles with stars, distant and bright, their energy dissipating silently through time and space.

the pin

AMONG MY MOTHER'S LETTERS I FIND A NOTE FROM MY FATHER. Written in the blue-black ink of his fountain pen are the words, in quotes, "A stone, a ———, a door." In place of the missing word are two holes in the piece of paper. But what is the quote, the missing word? A leaf! That's it. Thomas Wolfe. *Look Homeward, Angel.* I am excited by my discovery. But what about the two holes? And then it comes to me. My mother's secret space behind a wall in her office where things of special value were kept: passports, cash, keys, jewelry, legal papers and her father's microscope. I remember as a child she showed me a leaf-shaped pin she kept in a blue pouch. She told me that my father had given it to her in Stockbridge. I haven't seen it in nearly fifty years. I dream about it and then one day I find it as I open a box labeled "Important." All the things I remember seeing over the years as I stood with my mother peering into her secret cubby . . . And there, the little blue bag with a silver leaf pin. Intact, preserved, tarnished by time out of place. I bring it to my father's note and slide the clasp through the two little holes. It fits perfectly.

gift

I AM SIXTY YEARS OLD. I LOOK IN THE MIRROR AND I SEE BOTH of my parents. I look into my son's face and see myself. I unpack boxes of my parents' books, noting that in almost every book of my father's there is a picture postcard written to him by my mother or myself. Was that just a bookmark or something he left for me to find when I opened the book? There are still more boxes with letters and journals that will take me on more journeys. I hope I will finish before I die. Before time and memory swallow up my existence.

And then when I am gone, my son will come upon a photo of me taken at our house in San Francisco. I am eight years old. My parents are standing on either side of me. We are all squinting in the sun. I am holding a large toy horse. I have earned it for having conquered my car sickness. I am very happy and proud. He will remember that he has seen the horse in the kitchen of our house in Cambridge. He may even think that his smile looks like mine. Or maybe not.

" A stone, a , a door...."

The lost lane end into heaven has
been found, darling. The great forgotten
language has been remembered.

I love you.

ACKNOWLEDGMENTS

The following works are quoted within the text of this book:

Wheelis, Allen. 2006. *The Way We Are*. New York: W. W. Norton.

————. 1999. *The Listener*. New York: W. W. Norton.

————. 1992. *The Life and Death of My Mother*. New York: W. W. Norton.

————. 1980. *The Scheme of Things*. New York: Harcourt Brace Jovanovich.